Charles Dickens' Australia

Book Five
Maritime Conditions

W. P. Frith, R. A. R. Graves, A.R.A.

CHARLES DICKENS.

Charles Dickens' Australia

Selected essays from *Household Words* 1850–1859

Book Five

Maritime Conditions

Researched and presented by
Margaret Mendelawitz

SYDNEY UNIVERSITY PRESS

Published 2011 by SYDNEY UNIVERSITY PRESS
University of Sydney Library
sydney.edu.au/sup

Sydney University Press
Fisher Library F03
University of Sydney
NSW 2006 AUSTRALIA
Email: sup.info@sydney.edu.au

National Library of Australia Cataloguing-in-Publication entry

Mendelawitz, Margaret.
Charles Dickens' Australia : selected essays from Household Words 1850 - 1859 / maritime conditions / Researched and presented by Margaret Mendelawitz.
9781920899264 (pbk. : bk. 5)
9781920899271 (set)
Includes bibliographical references.
A823.4

Cover image: Hoisting main topsail by John Harold Graham, 1881. Image courtesy of National Library of Australia, nla.pic-an6442316.

Frontispiece: Portrait of Charles Dickens engraved by Robert Graves (1798–1873) after painting (1859) by William Powell Frith (1819–1909). Engraving published in the second volume of John Forster's *The Life of Dickens* (London: Chapman and Hall, 1872–74).

Cover design by Court Williams, University Publishing Service
Printed in Australia

Contents

Foreword vii
Introduction ix

Book Five: Maritime Conditions

Sentimental Geography 3
Short Cuts Across the Globe: [Panama Canal] 6
Short Cuts Across the Globe: [The Isthmus of Suez] 13
The Great Screw [Screw Propeller] 18
Two Adventures at Sea 27
Off to the Diggings! 37
Post to Australia 51
We Mariners of England 56
Sailor's Home Afloat 68
The Life of Poor Jack [Conditions of Seamen] 81
Chip: Voices from the Deep 91
Black-Skin Ahead! [Whaling] 93
Chip: The Treasures of the Deep 105

Contributors to *Household Words* 107
Bibliography 137

This book contains stories and articles written over 150 years ago, and from a predominantly Anglo-Celtic perspective. It contains terms and descriptions that we would not consider acceptable of people and cultural groups today. Women, the Irish, Chinese and Australian Aborigines are described in biased, racist, stereotypical or otherwise less than flattering terms. As Margaret Mendelawitz notes in her Introduction, Dickens himself held conservative views about women and their ability to overcome their 'lesser nature'.

We ask that you remember this as you read the stories, and encourage you to work towards a more positive understanding of the different groups that make up our community.

Foreword

The Australian gold rushes were, in the eyes of millions of Europeans of the 1850s, the most astonishing episode they could read about. Here was gold, lying on or near the surface of the ground in enormous quantities, and available to the first person who could dig a shallow hole with pick, crowbar and shovel. Some of the richest nuggets of gold ever found were on the Victorian goldfields. It was no wonder that emigration from the British Isles to this El Dorado was on an unprecedented scale.

The London magazine *Household Words* conveyed to thousands of literate homes the news and atmosphere, the strangeness and the excitement, of Australian daily life before and during the gold rushes. Two of the best writers living in Australia—they had arrived especially to dig gold or to watch it being dug—contributed prose and poems to *Household Words*. While the magazine had a focus far wider than this one country, it liked Australia to be one of its major themes.

Between 1850 and 1859 more than one hundred of its articles and many of its poems were about this country. At a time when Australia's white population was less than one million, and the local weeklies and monthlies were few and precarious, this high-circulation English magazine offered a freshly washed window on Australia. The window was unusual because it was controlled by the most celebrated English novelist, Charles Dickens. One of his novels, *Hard Times*, first appeared as a serial in this magazine. Dickens rewrote or edited many of the articles on Australian themes. Such was his fascination with this country that he encouraged or permitted his young sons to emigrate and take up pastoral lands. The older became a member of parliament in NSW, representing an outback seat.

Margaret Mendelawitz has collected, and given the background to, the prose and verse assembled here: she even knows how much the authors were paid, to the nearest shilling. We can see what English readers learned about Australia in those mid-century years: the long voyage and its dangers, the life of convicts and copper miners before the gold rushes, and the hazardous life in the bush: it published Louisa Meredith's long poem on the little child that disappeared. We experience through *Household Words* the jubilant streets of Melbourne when it was the busiest port for the new goldfields, the slow journey on foot to the diggings, the makeshift gold towns themselves, the life of migrating women at sea and on land, the eccentricities of the new-rich, and scores of other topics. Three stories—one of which is fictional but historically vital—hinge on the terrible bushfires of 6 February 1851. Known as Black Thursday it had virtually been wiped from the nation's collective memory before the bushfires of February 2009, Black Saturday resurrected it.

Some of these authors had not seen Australia but winnowed private letters and newspaper accounts. On the other hand 'Orion' Horne was the only English writer with a literary reputation who had settled here up to that time, and his stories of what he saw and heard are compelling. All in all, this is a rare anthology and mirror of Australia when it was glamorous and exotic for potential British emigrants, and enticed them here as never before.

Geoffrey Blainey
Melbourne, May 2010

Introduction
Margaret Mendelawitz

The articles, poems and narratives contained in this anthology were published by Charles Dickens in his weekly periodical, *Household Words*, between the years 1850 and 1859.

Today, Dickens is recognised as the foremost English novelist of the Victorian era, and at the time was probably the most famous writer in the English-speaking world. His many volumes include such works as *The Pickwick Papers, Oliver Twist, Martin Chuzzlewit, Bleak House, Great Expectations* and short stories such as the much-loved *A Christmas Carol.*

His first novel was published when he was in his mid-twenties and his reputation and standing as a writer continued to grow over the next thirty years. As a novelist Dickens was much more than a writer and entertainer. He was on one hand able to charm and delight his audience, while at the same time communicating his ideas on a great variety of subjects—often concerning ordinary people and frequently exposing the shortcomings and seamy nature of the lives of the poor, compared with the lives of the privileged.

He was also a natural journalist and enjoyed the power of being able to speak directly to his audience on subjects that concerned him. In the first edition of *Household Words,* published in England on 30th March 1850, he outlined its governing principles to be—'Principles of Progress and Improvements, of Education, Civil and Religious Liberty, Equal Legislation.'

Household Words proved to be a remarkable periodical that was published during an extraordinary decade in Australian and British history: a decade when the tumultuous effects of the discovery and mining of gold in New South Wales and Victoria were being experienced worldwide. In Britain and Australia the results of increasing attention to issues of social justice were being felt, and around the world, the 'age of capital' had begun.[1] Of the thousands of articles published in *Household Words* in this decade more than one hundred were related to Australia. It is these that are reproduced in this anthology.

Dickens was thirty-eight in 1850 when he began publishing *Household Words*. He had twice tried his hand as editor of other periodicals but had been frustrated by his lack of control over their content. Already an acclaimed author, he was also a journalist of twenty years experience. With a growing family to support, he saw *Household Words* as a way to generate a secure income whilst at the same time to allowing him to continue writing his novels. As a journalist, he had been a parliamentary reporter and had written on election campaigns and public meetings, as well as producing theatre reviews and reports of important dinners.[2] He was known for his 'comic, witty or punchy commentaries on topical subjects'—and in many ways, was a predecessor of today's magazine or newspaper columnist.

He had already proven himself to be a man of action. In 1839, at the age of twenty-seven, he met Baroness Angela Burdette Coutts, said to be the wealthiest woman in England after the Queen. They began to actively and enthusiastically cooperate in a wide-range of charitable projects, in particular *Urania Cottage* for the retraining and rehabilitation of fallen women.[3] Dickens was more practical and pragmatic in his approach than Baroness Coutts who was a promoter of abstinence, especially from sex and alcohol. He preferred to teach the women skills and to assist them to migrate to Australia to make a 'new start'. This approach would later on lead him to endorse the work of Caroline Chisholm in the first instalment of *Household Words*.[4]

By 1850, his views on social issues had become clearer and more radical. He announced the aim of *Household Words* as 'the raising up of those that are down, and the general improvement of our social conditions'.[5] His particular concerns were sanitation, education and housing, the lack of which he believed were the root causes of much of the 'disastrous conditions of England'. He was of the opinion that the causes of most of the ills of the world, including disease, crime and social unrest, were as a result of ignorance and neglect. This concern was a recurrent theme in Dickens' earliest writings.

However, his own attitudes were a mixture of conservatism and radicalism that persisted throughout his life. For instance, he was steadfastly conservative in his views regarding the place of women in society, where he maintained their natural place was firmly at home and other activities should not, in any way, take priority over the needs of the children. Indeed, he draws a metaphor to this in his novel *Bleak House*, (1853) with Mrs Jellyby, a do-gooder who neglects her children in order to do her charitable works. Mrs Jellyby is said to have been modelled on the social reformer Caroline Chisholm: yet, at the same time, he was endorsing Chisholm's charitable work in assisting families to emigrate to Australia. In addition, his own personal and family life was far from the virtuous model he projected as the ideal in his novels; he ultimately left his wife Catherine, taking their children with him, whilst maintaining a relationship with another woman, Ellen Ternan. His own travels, and the frantic pace of life he led, would, in today's society, constitute neglect of family duties.

Amongst humans, story is our unique and most powerful form of communication. It provides a window through which we can view the lives of others and so gain insight into their thoughts and subsequent actions. Topics can be introduced to readers in a range of ways aimed at informing them, raising their interest and fostering concern. Unconstrained, the story can move through time and place, linking the present with the past, engaging the reader at new emotional and experiential levels. By stimulating the imagination the well-constructed story facilitates contemplation and reflection on the human condition, in a way that indeed may be transformative.

Charles Dickens well understood the power of story. The narrative, more than simply providing entertainment for the reader (or listener), has the ability to transform: to enable the reader to enter the story and, moreover, for the story to enter the reader, often in a profound and lasting way. He also preferred the power of the popular press, rather than writing for the more scholarly publications. He wanted to be able to express important ideas by communicating through high-quality journalism in an inexpensive, readily available weekly.

Dickens wanted to affect, and hence change, the reader through story. He knew that hectoring and preaching more often had the effect of disengaging rather than engaging an audience. He wanted to enlighten and reform his society and to make a significant contribution to the cultural debate. He set out to do this by informative and influential storytelling, through the lively blending of fact and fiction, set against the realities of social conditions of the times.

Dickens disliked sermonising of any form and was especially repelled by religions that stressed adherence to dogma rather than compassion and goodwill—he was a man of religious convictions yet rarely went to church.[6] Dickens was by nature neither an ideologue nor a revolutionary. He was wary of trade unions while still sympathetic to the conditions of workers. Yet he believed in strict prison sentences rather than focusing on reform.

By 1850 he was already a man with a high profile having earlier taken a very public stand against the practice of public hangings. Dickens was appalled by the spectacle of public executions which had turned into a form of entertainment for the masses. When they were abolished in Britain in 1868 he was 'remembered as one of the great advocates of this change.'[7] He was against the social isolation of prisoners which he considered cruel and inhumane; and vehemently against slavery, which he had witnessed first-hand in America.[8] He considered that transported prisoners were virtually slave labourers and he strongly opposed this abuse.

Dickens had a great curiosity about other societies and other lands and had a great love of travel. He visited North America on two occasions and at various times had toured Italy, Switzerland, France, Ireland and Scotland. He published books on his American travels and on Europe. He was a keen observer of French culture, government and history and after his separation from his wife spent a large amount of his time living in France. His novel *A Tale of Two Cities* (1859) was set in France. Dickens' inquisitiveness and intense interest in faraway lands, including Australia, is mirrored in many of the articles in *Household Words*: it is also occasionally reflected in his novels when a character's fate was to find salvation in Australia, as did Magwitch in *Great Expectations* and Mr Micawber in *David Copperfield.*

Apart from providing the financial security Dickens was seeking, *Household Words* was to be a vehicle for promoting his ideas of reform and a way of forming a closer relationship with his readers. It was not to be a high-brow intellectual periodical. Above all he wanted to reach and entertain the masses and, at the same time, help shape discussion and debate on the important social questions of the time. His aim was to engage some of the best and most entertaining writers to produce a range of stories and narratives, as well as poetry—'good' poetry that would appeal to ordinary readers. However, Dickens' assessment of what was 'good' poetry was not always shared in educated circles.

The stories in *Household Words* were to have a clear purpose or focus which Dickens himself was to guide and influence. He intended to instruct, educate and assist the reader to make judgements on a very wide range of subjects. The articles were to be 'compilations' such as essays, reviews, letters, theatrical criticism, which were to be as 'amusing' as possible.[9] The writers were to be well paid, with a clear understanding of what was expected of them.

In setting down his governing philosophy for *Household Words,* and the range of subjects he wished to explore, Dickens wrote to his close friend and future biographer John Forster:

> Now to bind all this together, and to get a character established as it were which any of the writers may maintain without difficulty, I want to suppose a certain *Shadow* which may go into any place by sunlight, moonlight, starlight , firelight, candlelight, and be in all homes, and all nooks and corners, and be supposed to be cognisant of everything, and go everywhere, without the least difficulty. Which may be the theatre, the Palace, the House of Commons, the Prisons, the Unions, the Churches, on the Railroad, on the Sea, abroad and at home: a kind of semi-omnipresent, intangible creature. I don't think it would do to call the paper the The Shadow: but I want something tacked to that title, to express the notion of its being cheerful, useful, and always welcome Shadow.[10]

Beginning in March 1850, *Household Words* was published weekly for almost a decade. Publication ended in 1859 after a bitter quarrel with his publishers and shareholders in the enterprise, Bradbury and Evans. For the next ten years he published a similar periodical *All The Year Round (AYR)* until his death in 1870. However, *AYR* contained less political journalism and more serialised fiction. Dickens chose the ever competent William Henry Wills to be his principal subeditor of both *Household Words* and *AYR*—a capacity that Wills excelled in for nearly twenty years while carefully managing the day-to-day running of the periodicals. In addition to Dickens and his publishers, the other shareholders were John Forster and William Wills, both of whom wrote many articles for the periodical.

Dickens closely scrutinised each weekly publication, even while abroad, and wrote many of the articles himself. He was concerned that no inaccuracies crept into the pages, writing to Wills, 'nothing can be more damaging to *Household Words* as carelessness about facts. It is a hideous dullness'.[11]

Some of the pieces are what Dickens himself called 'composite' writings: materials he wrote in collaboration with other staff members. The final product was achieved by dividing the task and then flawlessly putting the sections together through meticulous editing. Dickens put an enormous amount of effort into refining the written works so that they appeared to be that of a single author. According to the Dickens scholar Harry Stone the result was that many of these articles are among the 'most carefully planned and polished writings' of Dickens' works.[12]

The same process applied to articles that had been submitted to him by writers who were not staff members or commissioned authors and to the few written by readers. The latter were often prefaced as 'Chip' which often commented on some aspect of a previous article. An example is the article 'Chip: Colonial Patriot',—an extract from a personal letter written to Dickens by John Fawkner, the first European to settle on the site of Melbourne in 1835. Occasionally a full-length article in the form of prose or poetry by a reader was published, but always after receiving a good buff-up from either Dickens or Wills to make it sparkle (and conform). It was not easy to have works published in *Household Words*: in 1854 for example, nearly 900 were submitted by readers and only were eleven printed.[13]

Included in this nucleus of staff writers were two who came to Australia during their time with *Household Words* with Dickens' instruction to send back articles for publication. They were Richard Horne, a salaried staff member who served with William Wills for a time as subeditor, and William Howitt. At another level, was a large group, many of whom were rising new writers at the time. They included Henry Morley, who was on the permanent staff with a salary of five guineas per week, and Samuel Sidney who was a regular contributor. Morley and Sidney both had brothers who spent time in Australia, and wrote articles for *Household Words*.

Other regular contributors included Wilkie Collins, Mrs Elizabeth Gaskell, and many others including Edmund Ollier, James Payn and George Sala, all prominent authors at the time. Though not permanent staff members, they augmented the team by writing on specialised subjects, such as science, medicine, legal matters, shipping and travel. Articles by Ollier, Payn and Sala are included in this anthology. George Sala also came to Australia long after Dickens' death and subsequently coined the aphorism 'Marvellous Melbourne'.[14] Beyond this level there was another group of writers including Elizabeth Barrett Browning, Dinah Maria Mulock, Edmund Yeats, and George Meredith; articles by the latter are included here.

Dickens was much more than editor-in-chief of *Household Words*, preferring to call himself the 'conductor' and he happily received letters and manuscripts addressed to Mr Conductor from hopeful writers from all around the world. By this means, Dickens maintained a direct linkage and close connection to his huge audience of readers—and they in turn provided the raw materials that so often shaped or informed the articles contained in the periodical. Also, and importantly, they informed the characters and settings appearing in his novels.

In addition, and essential for Dickens, he was now successfully able to promote his social concerns with the same action and energy as typified his narratives and novels. The audience was large. As Jane Smiley has said, in relation to his novels written at this time:

> He created a new sort of English novel, one that explores and questions the construction of English culture and society as a whole,

> rather than merely certain institutions. Dickens locates the dilemmas and tragedies of his characters in the institutions outside of their control and then analyses how some of the characters fail while others manage to cope.[15]

Except for the novel *Hard Times,* published in serial form in *Household Words*, it was not possible for Dickens to explore major themes in any depth in the short articles contained in *Household Words.* Nevertheless, at the outset Dickens had a clear vision as to the nature of the material to be included in the new periodical, writing to John Forster:

> Upon the selected matter, I have a particular notion. One is that it should always be *a subject.* For example … A history of Savages, showing the singular respect in which all savages are like each other; and those in which civilized men, under circumstances of difficulty, soonest become like savages. A history of remarkable characters, good and bad, *in* history; to assist the reader's judgement in his observation of men, and in his estimates of the truth of many characters in fiction.[16]

Of the nearly 3000 articles that appeared in *Household Words,* the narrative style was unashamedly middle-class in nature. It was deliberately pitched to capture the attention of the growing number of readers at this level of society. Each issue usually had between five and seven articles of popular interest, on topics such as sanitation, epidemics, education, the treatment of prisoners or children, or men at sea. Other themes covered were history, travel and literature. There was generally a story and an essay, and frequently a poem.

Most, if not all, were couched in a deliberately bright tone in which entertainment was combined with instruction. In an era when Victorian prudery and primness would not allow frank speaking about such things as sewage and filth, Dickens acceded to his public's sensitivities. He paid particular attention to style, and in everything, including the driest of subjects, he demanded brightness. His message once to his editor William Wills was to 'brighten it, brighten it, brighten it!' He also demanded the same from his writers, requiring them to adopt, as Mrs Gaskell termed, a

'Dickensy' style.[17] There was always a lead article each week that set the tone and shape of the articles to follow.

Another distinct characteristic was the provocative introductory paragraphs which were often deliberately clever, ingenious or snappy (often a pun) and intended to entice readers into articles containing serious messages. Dickens desired that the publication become 'the gentle mouthpiece of reform'.[18] As an indication of Dickens' control over subject matter, Martin Fido is very forthright, writing that throughout the life of the journal, Dickens 'could be and was—ruthlessly dictatorial on matters of content and style'. Furthermore, contributors who had not conformed to Dickens' views 'had their work re-written'[19] and regardless of their source, all articles appeared anonymously.

Household Words became extremely popular. It eventually averaged sales of about 40,000 copies per week and at its peak 100,000 copies per week, returning Dickens a good profit and secure income. In addition, he earned money from his novels, said to have been £11,000 from just one novel in the 1850s.[20]

Through *Household Words* Dickens had created the perfect vehicle of good humour and good spirits to reach even the poorest and most distant home. Many articles from *Household Words* were re-published in the Australian press. This was a further opportunity for Australians to see how they were being depicted in the popular press of the time, and conceivably, to influence the way Australians imagined themselves as a society. The reprinted articles would have communicated Dickens' views to a wider audience, providing Dickens with a unique opportunity to alter and shape public opinion in a progressive and rapidly developing country.

Of the articles reproduced in this volume, all are related in some way to Australia. What makes this collection unique is that they were all published between 1850 and 1859, the decisive decade in which gold was discovered in New South Wales and Victoria. These subsequent events were to not only to transform colonial Australia economically and socially, but changed how the colonies were perceived by the world at large.

To have so many articles published in one single periodical under the strict guiding hand of Charles Dickens is unparalleled in Australian literature. To have such a clear understanding of the guiding principles of the editor-in-chief is surely without precedent. Dickens obtained access to a wealth of knowledge from information and feedback from his Australian readership, as well as from his regular writers, such as Horne and Howitt. These staff writers, like so many people around the globe, were attracted to Australia by the excitement of gold. Thus, at the outset, they were commissioned by Dickens to record their journeys and their experiences for the readers of *Household Words*.

Many of these articles display a freshness and sense of drama we are familiar with today. But in a world where even Scotland was yet to be fully mapped (1862),[21] and with the interior of Australia unknown, uncharted and exotic, they were breaking new ground. They are, of course, not all eyewitness accounts. Many are representations based on fact, while some are serious critiques about shipping to Australia, 'We Mariners of England'; the plight of emigrants on board ships, 'A Diggers Diary'; or of living conditions in Melbourne, 'Canvass Town [sic]'. All are part of the body of literature that emerged with the gold rushes, literature that helped to shape a new way of thinking about life in colonial Australia. Australian life was now depicted as thrilling and different with an exciting future ahead, a country standing apart from its stark convict beginnings. Life in the new world was being presented as offering opportunities for a new start, radically different from that in early industrial Britain. Australia had just won the golden lottery, and the world was fascinated.

There are other snippets of information that make this collection so valuable. For example the amount each writer was paid varied: staff received a salary, while articles submitted regardless of the source were paid according to the piece and to the numbers of columns printed in the original publication. Interestingly poetry was always paid at a much higher rate than prose.

Biographical information about each of the contributors, including a list of their articles related to Australia, can be found at the end of the text; the biographies of each of the contributors providing yet another layer of insight into the articles. In many instances this is by no means a complete list of the writers' works, for many of these contributors wrote extensively for *Household Words* on subjects unrelated to Australia.

Of the thirty-five individual authors who contributed articles relating to Australia, by far the greatest proportion (twenty-one) had either lived in Australia for lengthy periods of time, or were permanent settlers. Of the latter, nine were either journalists or regular contributors to Australian publications, with two (Fawkner and Vincent) also colonial newspaper proprietors.

In addition, eight of the contributors published books about Australia—John Capper, Caroline Chisholm, William Howitt, John Lang, Louisa Meredith, brothers John and Samuel Sidney, and the Rev. William Ullathorne. In some instances, as in the case of John Lang, articles first published in *Household Words* formed the basis of a subsequent book.

Eric Hobsbawm has written in *The Age of Capital* that the coincidence of gold discoveries in California in 1848–49, and in Australia, marked the foundation of the 'global industrial economy' and the start of a 'single world history'.[22] Gold was the spark that ignited a sudden burst of mass migration, largely to America, and to a far lesser extent to Australia. Even so, in the space of ten years Australia's population trebled, while the population of Victoria rose by a factor of seven—a state of affairs unimaginable today.[23]

Gold transformed economies, created new markets and led to a world-wide economic surge. Australia, with the vast riches being claimed from its soil, was the powerhouse behind much of this. In the next decade this chain of events saw a new word, 'capitalism' entering into the economic and political vocabulary, and the growth and interdependence of the single world economy.[24]

As Geoffrey Blainey has written:

> In the year 1853 Australia bought 15 per cent of the total value of goods exported from Great Britain, the world's largest exporter. Britain's exports to the new gold countries of North America and Australia increased by 271 per cent in the years 1846–53; and in the same period Britain's exports to the rest of the world increased by only 21 per cent. There is evidence that California and then Australia had such purchasing power that they largely revived the sick economy of Britain, which in turn sent a chain reaction of prosperity around much of the civilized world.[25]

Apart from gold's great economic benefit, it was the prize that anyone with a bit of luck and capital might win. Australia benefited in many ways, but especially by the people it attracted, mostly young, physically fit men, frequently educated to some degree and willing to be adaptable, resourceful and to have a go! During the height of the gold rush up to 300 ships could be at anchor in Port Phillip Bay at any one time. Sailors deserted their ships and sea-going mates remained trusted mates at the diggings—thus helping to cement forever this term in the Australian idiom.

This melting pot of energetic young men from every class and rank of society helped to shape Australia's future politics. They helped to create a modern sense of justice, uncommon in their countries of origin, which revolutionised institutions and benefited the social and economic transition of Australia into a modern developing economy. This decade saw the granting of the eight-hour day for some workers and, in the decades to follow, manhood suffrage, payment for members of Parliament and the secret ballot; the list goes on.

Many of the articles published in *Household Words* capture the excitement of the times and many foreshadow the personal despair of hopeful immigrants. As a body of literature for the masses, *Household Words* does not set out to explore Australian society or culture as a whole. Very few articles reflect local politics but they do manage to highlight a range of issues, personal triumphs and tragedies reflecting the dramatic shift in the British perception of Australia in this extraordinary decade. Originally perceived to be a distant colonial outpost of convicts, farmers and squatters, Australia came to be depicted as a place of adventure, wealth and limitless future.

But these stories are literature, not history. They are historically enlightening and their value is in their ability to educate readers about the social and economic development of 19th-century Australia. This value does not depend on them being the literal truth, as even the most conscientious organising of facts will not necessarily convey absolute truth. What they do well is to show that there are all sorts of ways to express and develop important ideas—a concept which still holds resonance in today's multimedia society.

As a collection they demonstrate the complementary nature of storytelling between the writing of history and fiction. The stories in *Household Words* frequently draw a fine line between fact and fiction, giving voice to characters and events that could easily go unrecognised and unrecorded. In many ways they exemplify the fundamental problem encountered by historians through the ages of how to separate and present fact, fiction, myth and truth. Moreover, they demonstrate how to overcome the difficulties of bringing Australian history to life to make it more engaging, accessible and meaningful to the reader.

In their own way these articles aptly illustrate, through storytelling, that Australian history does not consist of a single narrative of events; they serve to illustrate that all history is in reality a rich layering of overlapping and often connected narratives, experienced by individuals, groups, communities and the nation as a whole.

Notes on Presentation of Articles

The topics included in this anthology are diverse. The articles have been subjectively placed into five general areas to make them more readily accessible. It is acknowledged that some of the articles may contain themes common to other sections; as much as possible they are organised chronologically and details of their date of publication are attached.

***Convict Stories* (Book One)** Conviction and court processes; conditions of prisons; and finally, treatment of convicts until conditional or final pardon received. The articles cover convicts on board ship, on Norfolk Island and mainland Australia and Tasmania, including prison hulks in Victoria.

***Immigration* (Book Two)** What to take to Australia and what to expect; where to get good information about immigration; how to choose a vessel to sail on.

***Frontier Stories* (Book Three)** Life in the bush. Farmers, squatters, explorers, Aborigines, bushrangers, cattle drives, floods, fire and other vignettes from everyday life.

Mining and Gold **(Book Four)** Copper mining in South Australia. How the discovery of gold beckoned people from all over the world to the gold diggings. The astonishing effect gold had on individuals the exploding population and colonial life in general. Stories of sailors deserting their vessels, Chinese immigrants and men and women of all ranks of society hoping to strike it rich. Life and death at the diggings, fashion and frivolity.

Maritime Conditions **(Book Five)** The need to improve the desperate conditions endured by seamen; the need for a faster route for ships to travel; steam ships; conditions on board for passengers on the long hazardous sea voyage to Australia. Also, a whaling story and much more.

Usually the original spellings and styles are retained. Occasionally the text has been altered in a small way, such as where spelling is inconsistent, for example when the archaic, trowsers and modern spelling of trousers is used interchangeably in one article, and when obvious typographical errors have occurred. Where 'pounds' was indicated as for instance 5*l*, instead of £5, it has been changed to be represented by the modern £ sign. Some of the very long paragraphs have been broken to assist the modern reader more used to shorter paragraphs, in each case the symbol ˜ has been inserted to indicate where the break occurs. Names of ships, newspapers and journals have been italicised. Now and then a word (or so) in square brackets has been added to aid comprehension.

While Dickens did not like footnotes to any degree (he referred to them as hiccoughs), there were a few in the original text which have been retained. In addition to these original footnotes a number of additional ones have been added for the benefit of the modern reader, such as, to define parts of ships, types of carriages and other modes of transport. Also, in the case where the word has little or no meaning in the modern context: for instance the use of the word plucks for offal.

Biographical notes for all contributors have been included at the end of each volume. These augment the reader's understanding of how Australia was being depicted in popular literature of the era. These biographical details reveal the rich diversity and depth of the Australian experience of the contributors.

Charles Dickens, 'The Conductor' had indeed chosen a remarkable group of individuals who successfully met his aims and hopes for *Household Words*.

Notes

[1] Hobsbawm, Eric, *The Age of Capital: 1848–1875*, p.13.
[2] Rosen, Michael, *Dickens: His Work and his World*, pp. 31–32.
[3] Smiley, Jane, *Charles Dickens*, p.18.
[4] Ackroyd, Peter, *Dickens*, pp. 617–23.
[5] Lohrli, Anne, *Household Words: Table of Contents*, p. 4.
[6] Murray, Brian, *Charles Dickens*, pp. 28–29.
[7] Fido, Martin, *Charles Dickens*. p. 74.
[8] Stone, Harry, *Charles Dickens' Uncollected Writings from Household Words*, pp. 433–42.
[9] Forster, John, *The Life of Charles Dickens: The Fireside Dickens*, p. 555.
[10] Forster, *ibid.*, p. 556.
[11] Ackroyd, Peter, *Dickens*, p. 623.
[12] Stone, *op. cit.*, p. 43.
[13] Hobsbaum, Phillip, *A Reader's Guide to Charles Dickens*, p. 128.
[14] Flannery, Tim, *The Birth of Melbourne*, p. 326.
[15] Smiley, *op. cit.*, p. 97.
[16] Forster, *op. cit.*, p. 555.
[17] Smiley, *op. cit.*, p. 92.
[18] Letter to Wills, March 6, 1850. cf., Una Pope-Hennessy, *Charles Dickens*, p. 302.
[19] Fido, *op. cit.*, p. 68.
[20] Ford, George H., *Dictionary of Literary Biography: University of Rochester*.
[21] Hobsbawm, Eric, *op. cit.*, p. 68.
[22] Hobsbawm, Eric, *op. cit.*, p. 63.
[23] Bate, Weston, *Victorian Gold Rushes*, pp. 8–9.
[24] Hobsbawm, Eric, *op. cit.*, p. 79.
[25] Blainey, Geoffrey, *The Rush That Never Ended*, p. 62.

"*Familiar in their Mouths as HOUSEHOLD WORDS.*"—SHAKESPEARE.

HOUSEHOLD WORDS.

A Weekly Journal.

CONDUCTED BY

CHARLES DICKENS.

VOLUME XIV.

FROM JULY 19, 1856, TO DECEMBER 27, 1856.

Being from No. 330 to No. 353, and also including the Extra Number and a half for Christmas.

NEW YORK:
DIX, EDWARDS & CO., 321 BROADWAY.
1856.

Book Five
Maritime Conditions

1
Sentimental Geography
Mr Irwin

Romantic fable of Abel Tasman, the Dutch explorer who named places he visited in Australia and New Zealand.
Volume: 8 Number: 192 Pages: 306–07
Date: November 26, 1853
Fee: 1 pound 1 shilling for 1 ¼ Columns.

Anthony Van Diemen, Governor of Batavia, had a daughter, whose name was Maria. Since she was not only charming and accomplished, but also the only child of a rich papa who was governor of the Dutch East Indies, Maria's image was impressed on many a heart, and she had no lack of suitors. There were great men among them; but, with maiden-like perversity, Maria most favoured a poor young sailor—a handsome, dashing fellow, who was very skilful in his business; but who had no pockets, or no use for any. The young sailor's name was Abel Jansen Tasman. He was devoted to Maria heart and soul, had exchanged pledges with her, and had brought matters to so serious a pass, that the proud father determined to put the young adventurer quietly and courteously out of sight: the doing so he took to be a better and more fatherly course than the institution of a great family quarrel. That his Maria should become Mrs. Tasman, he knew very well was a thing not for a moment to be thought of. Whoever won his daughter must have wealth and a patent of nobility. She was no fit mate for a poor sailor. Tasman, however, could be easily dismissed from dangling after her.

The Batavian traders had at that time a vague notion that there was a vast continent—an unknown Austral land somewhere near the South Pole; and Van Diemen determined to send Tasman out to see about it. If he never came back it would not matter; but, at any rate, he would be certainly a long time gone. Van Diemen therefore fitted out an expedition, and gave to young Tasman the command of it.

Off the young fellow set, in the year 1642, and, like an enamoured swain as he was, the first new ground he discovered—a considerable stretch of land, now forming a very well known English colony—he named after his dear love, Van Diemen's Land, and put Miss Van Diemen's Christian name beside her patronymic, by giving the name of Maria to a small adjoining island close to the south-eastern extremity of the new land. That land—Van Diemen's Land—we have of late begun very generally to call after its discoverer, Tasmania.

Continuing his journey southward, the young sailor anchored his ships on the eighteenth of December, in a sheltered bay, which he called Moodenare's (Murderer's) Bay, because the natives there attacked his ships, and killed three of his men. Travelling on, he reached, after some days, the islands which he called after the three kings, because he saw them on the feast of the Epiphany; and then, coming upon New Zealand from the north, he called it in a patriotic way, after the States of Holland, Staten Land; but the extreme northern point of it, a fine bold headland jutting out into the sea, strong as his love, he entitled again Cape Maria. For he had gone out resolved not indeed to 'carve her name on trunks of trees,' but to do his mistress the same sort of honour in a way that would be nobler, manlier, and more enduring.

After a long and prosperous voyage, graced by one or two more discoveries, Tasman came back to Batavia. He had more than earned his wife; for he had won for himself sudden and high renown, court favour, rank, and fortune. Governor Van Diemen got a famous son-in-law, and there was no cross to the rest of the career of the most comfortable married couple, Abel and Maria. Tasman did not make another journey to New Zealand; it remained unvisited until 1769, when it was re-discovered by Captain Cook, who very quickly recognised it as a portion of the land that had been first seen by the love-lorn sailor.

Notes

There were two ships on this voyage of discovery: Abel Janszoon Tasman (c.1603–1659) commanded the *Zeehaen* while the other, the *Heemskirk*, was under the command of Gerrit Jansz.

A very large element of historical romantic fiction has been injected into this article. Maria was not the daughter of the Governor-general of Batavia, Anthony van Diemen, but the governor's wife Maria Van Aelst.

Tasman was married twice. His first wife, Claesgie Meyndrix died in Holland leaving him with a young daughter. He married a second time to Jannetjie Tjaers (in January 1632). In 1638, she accompanied Tasman to Batavia, where he was then stationed. This was four years before he set out on to explore the waters of the southern Pacific in search of the South Land.

The story is a good example how historical mythology can develop. In this case, 26 years after its publication in *Household Words*, the Tasmanian writer Louisa Meredith, (and contributor to *H. W.* see biographical notes at end) repeated this fiction as fact in her 1879 writings on Tasmania, 'Our Island Home'.

2
Short Cuts across the Globe: [Panama Canal]
William Weir and W.H. Wills

The need for the Panama Canal.
Volume: 1 Number: 3 Pages: 65–68
Date: April 13, 1850
Fee: 2 pounds 12 shillings and 6 pence for 4 ¾ Columns.

To a person who wishes to sail to California an inspection of the map of the world reveals a provoking peculiarity. The Atlantic Ocean—the highway of the globe—being separated from the Pacific by the great western continent, it is impossible to sail to the opposite coasts without going thousands of miles out of his way; for he must double Cape Horn. Yet a closer inspection of the map will discover that but for one little barrier of land, which is in size but as a grain of sand to the bed of an ocean, the passage would be direct. Were it not for that small neck of land, the Isthmus of Panama (which narrows in one place to twenty-eight miles) he might save a voyage of from six to eight thousand miles, and pass at once into the Pacific Ocean. Again, if his desires tend towards the East, he perceives that but for the Isthmus of Suez, he would not be obliged to double the Cape of Good Hope. The Eastern difficulty has been partially obviated by the overland route opened up by the ill-rewarded Waghorn.[1] The western barrier has yet to be broken through.

Now that we can shake hands with Brother Jonathan in twelve days by means of weekly steamers; travel from one end of Great Britain to another, or

[1] Thomas Fletcher Waghorn (1800–1850): developed a new route from England to India via Egypt.

from the Hudson to the Ohio, as fast as the wind, and make our words dance to distant friends upon the magic tight wire a great deal faster—now that the European and Columbian Saxon is spreading his children more or less over all the known habitable world: it seems extraordinary that the simple expedient of opening a twenty-eight mile passage between the Pacific and Atlantic Oceans, to save a dangerous voyage of some eight thousand miles, has not been already achieved. In this age of enterprise that so simple a remedy for so great an evil should not have been applied appears astonishing. Nay, we ought to feel some shame when we reflect that evidences in the neighbourhood of both Isthmuses exist of such junctions having existed, in what we are pleased to designate 'barbarous' ages.

Does nature present insurmountable engineering difficulties to the Panama scheme? By no means: for after the Croton aqueduct, our own railway tunnelling and the Britannia tubular bridge, engineering difficulties have become obsolete. Are the levels of the Pacific and the Gulph of Mexico, which should be joined, so different, that if one were admitted the fall would inundate the surrounding country? Not at all. Hear Humboldt on these points.

Forty years ago he declared it to be his firm opinion that 'the Isthmus of Panama is suited to the formation of an oceanic canal—one with fewer sluices than the Caledonian Canal—capable of affording an unimpeded passage, at all seasons of the year, to vessels of that class which sail between New York and Liverpool, and between Chile and California.' In the recent edition of his 'Views of Nature,' he 'sees no reason to alter the views he has always entertained on this subject.' Engineers, both British and American, have confirmed this opinion by actual survey. As, then, combination of British skill, capital, and energy, with that of the most 'go-ahead' people upon Earth, have been dormant, whence the secret of the delay? The answer at once allays astonishment:—Till the present time, the speculation would not have 'paid.'

Large works of this nature, while they create an inconceivable development of commerce, must have a certain amount of a trading population to begin upon. A gold-beater can cover the effigy of a man on horseback with a sovereign; but he must have the sovereign first. It was not merely because the full power of the iron rail to facilitate the transition of heavy burdens had not been estimated, and because no Stephenson had constructed a 'Rocket engine,' that a railway with steam locomotives was not made from London to Liverpool before 1836. Until the intermediate traffic between these termini had swelled to a sufficient amount in quantity and value to bear reimbursement for establishing such a mode of conveyance, its execution would have been impossible, even though men had known how to set about it.

What has been the condition of the countries under consideration? In 1839, the entire population of the tropical American isthmus, in the states of Central-America and New Grenada did not exceed three million. The number of the inhabitants of pure European descent did not exceed one hundred thousand. It was only among this inconsiderable fraction that anything like wealth, intelligence, and enterprise, akin to that of Europe, was to be found; the rest were poor and ignorant aboriginals and mixed races, in a state of scarcely demi-civilisation.

Throughout this thinly-peopled and poverty-stricken region, there was neither law nor government. In Stephens's 'Central America,' may be found an amusing account of a hunt after a government, by a luckless American diplomatist, who had been sent to seek for one in Central-America. A night wanderer running through bog and brake after a will-o'-the-wisp could not have encountered more perils, or in search of a more impalpable phantom. In short, there was nobody to trade with. To the south of the Isthmus, along the Pacific coast of America, there was only one station to which merchants could resort with any fair prospect of gain—Valparaiso. Except Chile, all the Pacific states of South America were retrograding from a very imperfect civilisation, under a succession of petty and aimless revolutions. To the north of the Isthmus matters were little, if anything, better. Mexico had gone backwards from the time of its revolution; and, at the best, its commerce in the Pacific had been confined to a yearly ship between Acapulco and the Philippines. Throughout California and Oregon, with the exception of a few European and half-breed members, there were none but savage aboriginal tribes. The Russian settlements in the far north had nothing but a paltry trade in furs with Kamschatka, which barely defrayed its own expenses.

Neither was there any encouragement to make a short cut to the innumerable islands of the Pacific. The whole of Polynesia lay outside of the pale of civilisation. In Tahiti, the Sandwich group,[2] and the northern peninsula of New Zealand, missionaries had barely sowed the first seeds of morals and enlightenment. The limited commerce of China and the Eastern Archipelago[3] was engrossed by Europe, and took the route of the Cape of Good Hope, with the exception of a few annual vessels that traded from the sea-board States of the North American Union to Valparaiso and Canton. The wool of New South Wales was but coming into notice, and found its way to England alone round the Cape of Good Hope. An American fleet of whalers scoured the Pacific, and adventurers of the same nation carried on a desultory and inconsiderable traffic in hides with California, in tortoise-shell and mother of pearl with the Polynesian Islands.

What then would have been the use of cutting a canal, through which there would not have passed five ships in a twelvemonth? But twenty years have worked a wondrous revolution in the state and prospects of these regions.

The traffic of Chile has received a large development, and the stability of its institutions has been fairly tried. The resources of Costa Rica, the population of which is mainly of European race, is steadily advancing. American citizens have founded a state in Oregon. The Sandwich Islands have become for all practical purposes an American colony. The trade with China—to which the proposed canal would open a convenient avenue by a western instead of the present eastern route—is no longer restricted to the Canton river, but is open to all nations as far north as the Yang-tse-Kiang. The navigation of the Amur has been opened to the Russians by a treaty, and cannot long remain closed against the English and American settlers between Mexico and the Russian settlements in America. Tahiti has become a kind of commercial emporium. The English settlements in Australia and New Zealand have opened a direct trade with the Indian Archipelago[4] and China.

---

[2] Sandwich group: Hawaii.

[3] Eastern Archipelago: Indonesia.

[4] Indian Archipelago: modern day Malaysia and Indonesia.

Figure 5.1 Clipper ship *Marco Polo. Illustrated London News*, 19 February 1853.

The permanent settlements of intelligent and enterprising Anglo-Americans and English in Polynesia, and on the eastern and western shores of the Pacific, have proved so many *depôts* for the adventurous traders with its innumerable islands, and for the spermaceti whalers. Then the last, but greatest addition of all, is California: a name in the world of commerce and enterprise to conjure with. There gold is to be had for fetching. Gold, the main-spring of commercial activity, the reward of toil—for which men are ready to risk life, to endure every sort of privation; sometimes, alas! to sacrifice every virtue; one most especially, and that is Patience. They will away with her now.

Till the discovery of the new Gold country how contentedly they dawdled round Cape Horn; creeping down one coast and up another; but now such delay is not to be thought of. Already, indeed, Panama has become the seat of a great increasing and perennial transit trade. This cannot fail to augment the settled population of the region, its wealth and intelligence. Upon these facts we rest the conviction that the time has arrived for realising the project of a ship canal there or in the near neighbourhood.

That a ship canal, and not a railway, is what is first wanted (for very soon there will be both), must be obvious to all acquainted with the practical details of commerce. The delay and expense to which merchants are subjected, when obliged to 'break bulk' repeatedly between the port whence they sail and that of their destination, is extreme. The waste and spoiling of goods, the cost of the operation, are also heavy drawbacks, and to these they are subject by the stormy passage round Cape Horn.

Two points present themselves offering great facilities for the execution of a ship canal. The one is in the immediate vicinity of Panama; where the many imperfect observations which have hitherto been made, are yet sufficient to leave no doubt that, as the distance is comparatively short, the summit levels are inconsiderable, and the supply of water ample. The other is some distance to the northward. The isthmus is there broader, but is in part occupied by the large and deep fresh-water lakes of Nicaragua and Naragua. The lake of Nicaragua communicates with the Atlantic by a copious river, which may either be rendered navigable, or be made the source of supply for a side canal. The space between the two lakes is of inconsiderable extent, and presents no great engineering difficulties. The elevation of the lake of Naragua above the Pacific is inconsiderable; there is no hill range between it and the Gulph of Canchagua; and Captain Sir Edward Belcher carried his surveying ship *Sulphur* sixty miles up the Estero Real, which rises near the lake, and falls into the gulf. The line of the Panama Canal presents, as Humboldt remarks, facilities equal to those of the line of the Caledonian Canal. The Nicaragua line is not more difficult than that of the canal of Languedoc, a work executed between 1660 and 1682, at a time when the commerce to be expedited by it did not exceed—if it equalled—that which will find its way across the Isthmus; when great part of the maritime country was as thinly inhabited by as poor a population as the Isthmus now is; and when the last subsiding storms of civil war, and the dragonnades of Louis XIV., unsettled men's minds and made person and property insecure.

The cosmopolitan effects of such an undertaking, if prosecuted to a successful close, it is impossible even approximatively to estimate. The acceleration it will communicate to the already rapid progress of civilisation in the Pacific is obvious. And no less obvious are the beneficial effects it will have upon the mutual relations of civilised states, seeing that the recognition of the independence and neutrality in times of general war of the canal and the region, through which it passes, is indispensable to its establishment.

We have dwelt principally on the commercial, the economical considerations of the enterprise, for they are what must render it possible. But the friends of Christian missions, and the advocates of Universal Peace among nations, have yet a deeper interest in it. In the words used by Prince Albert at the dinner at the Mansion House respecting the forthcoming great Exhibition of Arts and Industry, 'Nobody who has paid any attention to the particular features of our present era, will doubt for a moment that we are living at a period of most wonderful transition, which tends rapidly to accomplish that great end—to which indeed all history points—the realisation of the unity of mankind. Not a unity which breaks down the limits and levels the peculiar characteristics of the different nations of the earth, but rather a unity the result and product of those very national varieties and antagonistic qualities. The distances which separated the different nations and parts of the globe are gradually vanishing before the achievements of modern invention, and we can traverse them with incredible speed; the languages of all nations are known, and their acquirements placed within the reach of everybody; thought is communicated with the rapidity, and even by the power of lightning.'

Every short cut across the globe brings man in closer communion with his distant brotherhood, and results in concord, prosperity, and peace.

3

Short Cuts across the Globe: [The Isthmus of Suez]

William Weir and W.H. Wills

The need for the Suez Canal.
Volume: 1 Number: 7 Pages: 167–68
Date: May 11, 1850
Fee: 2 pounds for 3 ½ Columns.

That little neck of land which lies between the head of the Red Sea and the Gulf of Gaza, in the Mediterranean, is the cause of merchandise circumnavigating the two longest sides of the triangular continent of Africa on its way to the East; instead of making the short cut which is available for passengers by what is called the 'overland route.' If a water-way were opened across the Isthmus, the highway for the goods traffic as well as for the passenger traffic of Europe, India, China, and Australia, will be along the Mediterranean and Red Seas and the Indian Ocean. And that highway will be so thronged, that the expense of travelling by it will be reduced to a *minimum*, and the accommodations for travellers at intermediate stations raised to a *maximum* of comfort.

This state of affairs—analogous to that which occurs in the intercourse of two towns where there is a round-about road for carts and carriages, and a footpath across the meadows for foot-passengers only—is attended by great inconveniences. Letters relating to mercantile transactions are forwarded by the short cut; the merchandise to which they relate follows tardily by the round-about road. The advantageous bargain concluded now may have a very different aspect when the goods come to be delivered three or four months hence. The seven-league-boot expedition of letters, and the tardy progress of goods, converts all transactions between England and India into a game of chance. This fosters that spirit of gambling speculation already too rife among us.

Again, so long as the route for passengers continues to be something different and apart from the route for merchandise, the travelling charges will be kept higher, and the accommodations for travellers less comfortable than they would otherwise be. Railways, in arranging their tariff of fares, venture to reduce the charge for passengers (in the hope of augmenting their number) when they can rely upon the returns from the goods traffic to make up deficiencies. If merchandise, as well as travellers and letters, could be carried by what is called the overland route (of which scarcely two hundred miles are travelled by land), the passengers' fares would admit of great reduction; and as that route would thus become the great highway, frequented by greater crowds, the accommodation of travellers could be better cared for. Travellers in carriages rarely reflect how much the amount of charges at inns depends upon the landlords having a profitable run of business among less distinguished guests.

As we remarked, when descanting on the Panama route, physical obstacles to the opening of short cuts are of much less consequence than those which originate in financial difficulties. Almost any physical obstacles may be overcome, if money can be profitably invested in the undertaking, and if money can be got for such investment.

Were we projectors of companies, and engaged in preparing an attractive prospectus, we might boldly declare that the obstacles in the construction of a ship canal at Suez are trifling, and that the work would prove amply remunerative. But being only impartial spectators, we are obliged to confess that our information respecting the nature of the country is lamentably defective, and that what we do know does not warrant any sanguine expectation. Public attention has been industriously directed from the true line of a ship canal across the Isthmus of Suez. The late Mehemet Ali[1]—peace to his ashes!—was a humbug of the first water, and he knew how to avail himself of the services of kindred spirits. He understood enough of European

[1] Mehemet Ali Pacha (1769–1849): Viceroy of Egypt who is often cited as the founder of modern Egypt.

whims and sentiments to know what tone of language he must adopt in order to persuade Europeans he was subserving their views, while he was, in reality, promoting his own. He talked, therefore, of facilitating the intercourse between India and Europe, but he thought of making that intercourse pass through his dominions by the longest route, and in the way which would oblige travellers to leave the greatest possible amount of money behind them; and to attain his ends he retained in his service a motley group of Europeans—the vain, the ignorant, and the jobbing, who did his spiriting after a fashion that bears conclusive testimony to his judgment and tact in selecting them.

What is really wanted for the commerce of Europe and India is a ship canal across the Isthmus of Suez, by the shortest and least difficult route. What Mehemet Ali conceded was a land passage through his dominions by the longest possible route. The natural course of a ship canal is, in a straight line, from Suez to the eastern extremity of Lake Menzaleh: the line of transit conceded by Mehemet Ali is from Alexandria by Cairo to Suez, nearly three times as long. The former line passes across a low and well-watered region: the latter renders necessary an interchange of canal and river navigation, and dry land passage across the desert. The former might be passed in a day without halting: the latter occupies several days, and includes necessary stoppages in the inns of Alexandria and Cairo. But Mehemet Ali and his tools directed attention from the former, and gabbled about railways and other impracticabilities, and the European public was gulled. Egypt can be reached any day by a fortnight's easy and luxurious travel, and yet the country between the eastern extremity of Lake Menzaleh and Suez is less accurately known than the Isthmus of Panama.

What we do know, with any degree of certainty about this transit, is briefly as follows:—The navigation of the Red Sea in the vicinity of Suez is rather intricate, abounding in shoals, but there is secure anchorage, and sufficient draft of water for merchant ships of considerable burden. The Mediterranean off the eastern extremity of Lake Menzaleh is rather shallow, tolerably sheltered from the west wind, which prevails for a part of the year, but exposed to the north wind. Between Suez and the site of the ruins of Pelusium at the eastern end of the lake, the land is low and level, apparently for a part of the way between the levels of both seas. The low land receives in the wet season the drainings of the high land on the east, which is a northern continuation of the mountains between the gulfs of Suez and Akaba. In addition to this, the land to the westward (northward of the Mokattam Mountains which terminate near Cairo) has a twofold slope,—the principal northward to the Mediterranean, the secondary eastward to the line of country we are now describing. Originally, there appears to have been a branch of the Nile entering the Mediterranean near where the ruins of Pelusium now are, and those intermediate branches between that and the Damietta branch.

The first mentioned is now closed, the other two very much obstructed; but their waters still find a way to the coast, though diminished by artificial works, and appear to be the cause of the collection of shallow water called Lake Menzaleh. Here, then, we have sixty geographical miles of a low country, with no considerable undulations, towards which the waters of Arabia Petræa flow in their season, and towards which a considerable portion of the waters of the Nile would flow if left to fall on the natural declivity of the country. There is an abundant supply of water for a ship canal. The surface of the ground is in some places covered with drift sand, but not uniformly nor even for the most part. The subsoil is hard, clayey or pebbley. The bent-grasses might be cultivated, as they have been in Holland, to give firmness to the drift sand where it occurs; and this superficial obstacle removed, the subsoil is favourable to the construction of a permanent water-channel. The great difficulty would be the construction of works by which access to the canal is to be obtained from the Mediterranean. Apparently they would require to be carried far out into the sea; and apparently it would be difficult to prevent their being sanded up by the waves which the north winds drive upon the coast for a great part of the year.

These difficulties, though great, are not insuperable. The advanced state of marine architecture and engineering ought surely to be able to cope with them. By re-opening the Pelusiac branch of the Nile, and throwing into it the waters which would naturally find their way into the Tanitic and Mendesian branches, a sufficient stream of water might be thrown into the Mediterranean at Pelusium to keep a passage open by its *scour*. We must speak with diffidence about a locality which has yet been so imperfectly surveyed; but so far as the present state of our knowledge respecting it enables us to judge, there are no serious impediments to the construction of a ship canal from Pelusium to Suez, which would be perfectly accessible and practicable for vessels of from 300 to 350 tons burden; and there is a growing impression among merchants and skippers that this class of vessels is the best for trading purposes.

But the great difficulty remains yet to be noticed; the condition of government and civil security in that country. The isthmus is close on the borders of civilised Europe, and ample supplies of effective labourers could be procured from Malta, and the Syrian and African coasts. But so long as the country is subject to a Turkish dynasty, could the undertakers count upon fair play and sufficient protection from the local authorities? And are the jealous powers of Europe likely to combine in good faith to afford them a guarantee that they should be enabled to prosecute their enterprise in security?

4
The Great Screw [Screw Propeller]
John Capper

Following the introduction of the screw propeller global shipping routes were transformed. This was especially so for steam shipping to Australia and New Zealand.
Volume: 8 Number: 187 Pages: 181–84
Date: October 22, 1853
Fee: 3 pounds 13 shillings and 6 pence for 6 ½ Columns.

When Mr. Hargreaves rode into Sydney with a small piece of gold and quartz-rock in his pocket, he could scarcely have understood that he carried with him that which would not only change the destinies of the great Australian continent, but likewise affect to a large extent a revolution in the commercial relations of the whole civilised world. And when, on the first of May eighteen hundred and fifty-one—the very day on which our Great Exhibition in Hyde Park was opened—the Governor of New South Wales penned his official sanction to the gold explorer's further labours, neither of them can have pictured a tithe of the mighty results which were destined to originate from that one epistle—

'What great events from trifling causes spring!'

Few things of moment have had more insignificant beginnings than the screw propeller for steam-ships; and few inventions are destined to produce more important benefits, more especially in connection with the great gold results which have sprung from Mr. Hargreaves's trifling nugget. The Australians can no more get on without the potent aid of the screw, than they can do without cradles, dampers, wide-awakes,[1] Guernsey shirts, and patent revolvers. The screw will bring them within a fifty-five days' run of home. The screw will drive their gold to the markets of Europe more safely and expeditiously than any other propeller. The screw will enable their 'made men' to reach the mother country without a gale or a fit of sea-sickness, by cheating both the much dreaded Capes. The screw is, in fact, the Australians' 'coming machine.'

Many of the most valuable scientific improvements have been brought to light by unexpected agencies. Amongst the hundred and fifty patents which have been taken out for various applications of the screw propeller, may be found, in addition to the names of engineers, machinists, ship-builders, and other professional men, those of ropemakers, farmers, printers, wharfingers, merchants, soldiers, and noblemen; and it is an undoubted fact that the most valuable additions made to our stores of screw-knowledge, have come from men uneducated for, and unconnected with, any branch of practical engineering. Whilst machinists and civil engineers had for fifty years failed to contrive any really practical adaptation of the screw for propulsion, the laurels of screw science were won, first in seventeen hundred and ninety-four by a merchant, and since, in eighteen hundred and thirty-six, jointly by an English farmer and a Swedish military officer.

The first attempt at screw propelling, which in any degree realised its object, was that of Mr. Lyttleton, a merchant of Goodman's Fields. It was, however, too rude and inefficient for practical purposes, and was laid aside with scores of other useless projects which saw the light between that period and the year eighteen hundred and thirty-six. One single exception to this array of failures is to be found in the improvement of a Mr. Cummerow, also a merchant of London; who, in eighteen hundred and twenty-nine, placed the screw between the stern of the ship and the rudder-post, a principle which has been since adhered to.

Early in the spring of eighteen hundred and thirty-six, Mr. J. P. Smith, a farmer of Hendon, obtained a patent for a new screw propeller; and so well did he succeed in working his first little model exhibited at the Adelaide

[1] Wide-awakes: a soft felt hat with a low crown and a high brim.

Gallery, that he obtained assistance which enabled him to build and fit up a small vessel of six tons. During the month of November of the following year, the screw-propelling farmer ventured out to sea in his toy-ship; and proceeded boldly down Channel, making excellent progress through a stormy sea, and dead against the wind. So complete was the triumph of the screw, that all the scientific world were convinced; and even the Admiralty found ears to listen. A larger vessel was consequently built, in which many of the naval authorities made experimental trips to sea and round the English coast; with such success, that eventually Government formally adopted the new propeller, and laid down the Rattler of eight hundred and eighty-eight tons, to be fitted with engines and a powerful and improved screw. By this time an accident which happened to the first wooden model, demonstrated that a short screw, with narrow fans, was better than a long screw with broad fans; and the iron screw made for the Rattler was of a double thread, but of only one-sixth of a convolution. A year or two later, the principle was so completely established in the royal dockyards, that twenty ships of war were fitted with auxiliary screw-power.

While Smith had been thus active, Ericsson, a Swedish officer, had also laid before the authorities a screw of a novel construction; but, however well this may have been worked experimentally, the Government were not at that time disposed to think favourably of the new propeller, and Ericsson carried his patent to the United States, where he also improved on Stirling's hot air engine, but only with partial success. The latest and most valuable advance in the construction of screw propellers, is that made by Mr. Griffiths: which—by a modification of the breadth of each section of the curved thread, by altering the size and shape of the screw's centre, and not less by an ingenious contrivance for 'feathering' the blades, and diminishing or increasing their pitch or slope at will—was greatly added to the value of screw machinery.

The merchant service and public companies have equally availed themselves of the invention; and, at the present time, some of the largest ships afloat are screw-propelled. Indeed, so marked are the advantages of the screw over the paddle, that there is little doubt but that the former will eventually be superseded, except in navigating shallow water; and that a paddle steamer across the ocean will, twenty years hence, be as rare an object as a stage coach on the high roads of Britain.

Having thus sketched the progress of Screw Steam Navigation, a short space will suffice for an explanation of what this screw consists, how placed, and in what its great advantages reside. The reader will no doubt gladly be spared a treatise on the resistance of fluid bodies, on the true pitch and disc of screw propellers, on positive and negative slip, or centrifugal action. It may be enough to say, that the screw-propellers now most commonly in use are what are termed double-threaded, of about one-sixteenth of a convolution; in plainer language, they consist of two twisted iron blades fixed upon a shaft revolving beneath the water, at the stern. This shaft is surrounded by a stuffing-box with hemp packing, to keep the aperture in the ship's stern watertight; its extremity is set in a socket attached to the rudder-post. The screw itself revolves in that part of the stern of the ship called the *Deadwood*, in which a suitably sized hole is cut to admit of its working. It is the thrust, or forward pressure of the blades, or sections of the screw threads, which is effective in propelling the ship.

Numerous trials as to the relative qualities of the paddle and the screw have resulted in a most complete demonstration of the superiority of the latter as an auxiliary power to vessels under canvas. For long sea-voyages in which calms, light airs, or fair breezes are looked for, a screw ship of fifteen hundred tons and three hundred horse power, would be preferable in point of speed and economical working to a paddle steamer of the same size and of three times the horse power. It has been clearly shown that a screw steamer makes as much way under canvas and with half steam on, as without sails and with her whole steam power applied. Indeed, wherever sails can be used at all, the advantages of the screw appear most clearly: even in sailing close-hauled to the wind, a vessel by the aid of the screw may be propelled four knots, when previously only making one knot an hour.

Experiment has demonstrated that an auxiliary screw-power sufficient to propel a ship not more than a mile or a mile and a half an hour, when brought to the aid of the sails, has in reality added three or four miles an hour to her speed. This is accounted for in the following manner:—when the vessel is propelled by canvas alone, and at a low rate of sailing, the wind quickly rebounds from the sails, and forms a sort of eddy or dead air in their rear, which acts to an extent adversely; for the sails do not receive nearly the whole advantage of the breeze; but, the moment more speed is imparted by auxiliary power, the sails retain the wind longer, having more of it, and there is not the same degree of rebound. In like manner the sails assist the action of the screw, by enabling it to work upon a larger surface of water, and so extend its power.

It is evident, therefore, that except in running against a head gale, the screw-propelled ship must have the advantage. In regard to the original cost and working the two kinds of steamers, there is an enormous difference. Calculations show that the relative expense of the three classes of ships is as nine for paddle-steamers, to four for sailing-vessels and three for auxiliary screw-ships.

Looking to these advantages, it is highly interesting to examine in what direction screw steamers fitted on the auxiliary principle, are most likely to prove of the greatest utility.

It was a happy circumstance that, coeval with the extension of the British possessions in that most remote part of the earth, the great south land of Australia, the screw principle should have been brought forward as a means of economising the use of fuel. By any of the routes to the colonies of Australia, the voyage, out and home, of a sailing vessel has been to the present time a most tedious and unpleasant affair. It is true there are Marco Polos, and Flying Dragons, and Sovereigns of the Seas which have made rapid passages with sails alone; but we all know what the old adage tells us about one swallow not making a summer. An average taken from the voyages of six hundred vessels, out and home, in 'thirty-nine and 'forty-nine, gives one hundred and thirty-four days as the outward run in the former year, and one hundred and nineteen days for the latter; whilst, for the homeward voyage, they were one hundred and fifty-one and one hundred and twenty-eight days. In 'forty-nine, the longest passage made to Port Phillip was one hundred and eighty-six days; the shortest, one hundred and one days.

This is tedious work; knocking about is calms, gales of wind, and adverse breezes, during those one hundred and eighty-six days, with the biscuit green and wormy, and the water looking like bad pea-soup, smelling of stale rum casks and tasting of logwood and rusty nails. Still it did not much signify when emigrants were few; when the homeward-bound with fortunes were still fewer; and when the great bulk of the cargoes from those countries consisted of wool, tallow, and copper-ore. The golden dream of Hargreaves in eighteen hundred and fifty-one, has become a splendid reality in eighteen hundred and fifty-three; and a community, suddenly converted from shepherds, shopkeepers and convicts, to capitalists, landholders, and bankers, demands some more rapid means of communicating with Europe than the colliercraft hitherto employed in the trade to Australia.

Two years ago a Committee of the House of Commons made an inquiry and published a report upon the subject of communication with the Australian colonies. Three routes were proposed to the committee, and evidence adduced on behalf of them all. These consisted of—first, the present overland route to India, with a branch line of steamers to ply between Singapore and Sydney; secondly, direct communication with the colonies by way of the Cape of Good Hope; and thirdly, a line proposed by a new steam-packet[2] company, to run more directly than either of the other routes, across the Isthmus of Panama, across the Pacific Ocean by way of New Zealand to Sydney and Melbourne. The two former were adopted by the Government authorities for the mail service; nevertheless so convinced were the projectors of the Australian Pacific Mail Steam-Packet Company of the superiority of the Panama line, that a fleet of six iron steam-ships of two thousand tons and fitted with powerful screw engines were at once laid down. Two of them are already launched.

The Cape and India lines have been working for some time, and the result of their operations furnishes the best answer to any speculations on the subject as far as speed is concerned. By way of Singapore the mail contract to Sydney has been performed in eighty-three days, and homewards it has been accomplished in eighty-nine and eighty-six days. The Cape contract has been still more unfortunate, the ships in that service having occupied between ninety-four and one hundred and twenty days outwards; and, on the

[2] Packet ship: a ship travelling on regular routes carrying mail, freight and a small number of passengers.

homeward run, something more. The above work has been performed by paddle steamers, and certainly offers no advantages over some of the improved sailing vessels which now make the run in eighty to ninety days.

Although it is thus shown that the Peninsular and Oriental Company's vessels have failed in opening a rapid communication with the southern and eastern ports of Australia, they have unquestionably achieved great success on the Indian line: what they have performed on the Suez route to Calcutta, the Australian Pacific Company will in a few more months accomplish by means of the Isthmus of Panama and the Pacific, for Melbourne and Sydney.

By no means the least important feature in this new route is the existence of extensive coal-fields in New South Wales and New Zealand; existing as if expressly to further the great scheme which is now being matured of encircling the world with a chain of iron and steam. Looking at the relative positions of Australia, Panama, and England, it cannot fail to be evident that no difficulty will be experienced in keeping up a regular monthly and even fortnightly communication, in about forty-five days. Time is the one great consideration in all business transactions, and it is difficult to over-estimate the effects of thus bringing our friends in the golden colonies so near home as to enable us to receive replies to our letters in something over a hundred days, or in less time than it now requires to convey a letter outwards by some of the steamers by way of the Cape. The accomplishment of this must constitute the Pacific route the great post-road to Australia—the highway for passengers, as well as the main gold channel thence to this country.[3] The Australian merchants will economise a large sum annually by the saving of interest on the value of the gold sent by this line—the result of bringing it home in fifty-five days, instead of eighty or ninety days as at present. This saving upon only half the yield of the Australian gold-fields would amount to a very considerable sum; thus verifying the axiom, that 'Time is money.'

From Southampton to the Atlantic side of the Panama Isthmus, the service will be performed by the Royal Mail Steam-Packet Company, which is now building five new vessels of great speed and accommodation. They are

---

[3] [Original footnote] See 'Short Cuts Across the Globe.' *Household Words,* Vol. 1, p. 65 [see also p. 6 in this volume].

intended to ply in connexion with the ships already running to the West Indies. Arrived at Panama, the outward-bound traveller will find a railway ready, with all its appliances, to whisk him off across the narrow band of earth (forty-nine miles in breadth) which separates the two great waters of the world. This line will be opened for traffic early in the ensuing year, twenty miles of it being already in operation, and steam will thus sink the distance into utter insignificance.

The shortness of this route is, however, not its only recommendation. The fair winds, the placid sea, the beautiful climate, all point to it as one that will be traversed in far more comfort and bodily enjoyment than any other. From January to December an unceasing monsoon wind blows across the South Pacific, always available, and, for auxiliary screw steamers, the finest breeze that could prevail. This would indeed appear to be the best field in which the many advantages of Screw Steam Navigation could be shown. With an eight knot breeze and all canvas spread, the Black Swan or the Emu iron steamers, aided by half steam power, may bound across that unruffled ocean, with a speed realizing the flight of their living name-sakes across the great Australian prairies. It was this delightful region which enchanted the earliest English and French navigators: it was here the adventurous Cook spent many weeks of his ocean life: and it was from this part of the Pacific that the author of Typee and Omoo drew the materials for his interesting tales.

For the return voyage, winds, nearly as favourable, are to be found by steering well to the southward for a short time after leaving the Australian continent. In these latitudes westerly breezes blow for a great part of the year, which will not fail to carry a vessel to the South American coast in fair weather. A screw vessel need not make the American coast; but, by steering towards the north, when within a certain distance of land, the Isthmus of Panama will be easily made. It should be borne in mind that, during the whole voyage, there is one continuous summer breeze and summer sky; not a cloud dims the bright blue of the tropical horizon; the unruly wave seldom troubles the face of the well-named Pacific. By this route the passengers need fear no storms; no heavy squalls of wind or rain; no unpleasant motion of the ship. The terrors of the much dreaded 'Cape of Storms' are escaped equally with the piercing cold of Cape Horn in a voyage which the most delicate and nervous may undertake without fear or inconvenience.

Whether the great ship-canal which is promised to connect the Atlantic and Pacific Oceans will be realised, or whether the Panama railway continue to be the means of transit across the Isthmus, will not affect the certain and speedy success of the 'great screw' question in a region which, of all others, appears to be the best adapted to a mode of propelling ships, which is at once economical, rapid, and agreeable.

5
Two Adventures at Sea
Samuel Sidney

Tales of maritime adventure and derring-do.
Volume: 2 Number: 31 Pages: 104–08
Date: October 26, 1850
Fee: 3 pounds for 7 Columns.

Having made up my mind to sail for Australia, my next care was to select a vessel. They were not so plentiful, so punctual, or so much puffed as they are now. For want of knowing any better, and partly from a dislike to crowds that has always been part of my character, and perhaps did much toward making me happy in the Bush when friends and companions of the same age were miserable, I took a passage in a small, fast-sailing brig,[1] under two hundred tons burden, which was intended to be sold for a coaster in the colony. The captain was going out to settle; he took his wife with him, but I was the only passenger. Captains on shore and captains at sea are quite different creatures. This was one of the old school. On shore, he seemed like a jolly fellow, rough and good-natured—at sea, he was a perfect brute, got drunk every evening, thrashed his wife, and ill-used his men; but, although profoundly ignorant on most subjects, a thorough seaman.

On the morning we were to sail, we lay in the stream of the Mersey, Blue Peter[2] flying and anchor tripped; we waited for the captain and mate so long, it seemed as if we should miss the tide. At length he came, as fast as two pair

[1] Brigantine: a vessel with two masts, square-rigged sails.
[2] Blue Peter: blue signal flag with a white square in the centre used to indicate that a merchant vessel is ready to sail.

of oars could pull him, looking very red and angry; no mate, but a strange man sitting in the stern sheets beside him. It seemed the mate had given him the slip at the last moment, and he had been obliged to engage the stranger, with very little enquiry. This man was a, lanky north country man, with a deadly pale face, without whiskers, a bald forehead, an immense mouth, black eyes, with an awful squint, and a costume of seedy black, so that he looked much more like a hedge schoolmaster than a sailor. He carried a parcel of sea-faring clothes in his hand, which the captain had been obliged to buy for him at the nearest slopshop.[3] He brought nothing else, but a large very light chest, and an enormous appetite. But, in spite of his unprepossessing appearance, and shore-going costume, the crew at once recognised him as a regular sea-dog. Indeed, by the time he got into his pea-coat and loose trowsers, and had a fortnight of our fare, if he did not grow handsomer, he seemed, at any rate, transformed into the style of man that attracts thunders of applause in a minor theatre as a wicked pirate. At least, that was my impression when, after a fortnight's landsman's misery, I crept on deck in the Bay of Biscay,[4] to see the 'seas' not 'in mountains rolling,' but as still as a mill-pool; and our mate, Mr. Clank, his complexion very much improved by sea air and salt water, taking his turn at the helm, in regular 'old salt style.'

I have now made the long sea voyage half-a-dozen times, and have come to the same conclusion I did at the end of my first—that there are very few who can do much real work at sea. On shore it is very easy to prepare journals, plan a course of study, lay in a store of scientific books, but when once you get into blue water, your berth becomes a very Castle of Indolence. What with sea-sickness, and the appetite that follows your recovery, you find your time pretty well consumed by eating, drinking, smoking, and dozing, relieved by reading a novel or playing a game at cards. There are exceptions, as, perhaps, on board a yacht, where you can go ashore when you please; but,

---

[3] Slops: loose covering garment for workmen—smock, apron or overall.

[4] Bay of Biscay: situated on the coast of France (from Brest south to the Spanish border) and along the northern coast of Spain.

as a general rule, gossip and brandy-and-water are the two great resources of a long voyage—more shame to the weakness of the passengers.

For my part, by the time I got my sea-legs I had every inducement to study, for the captain and his wife were no companions to me. I did read my store of books twice over, learned to splice a rope, and, after a fashion, to hand, reef, or steer; had a good deal of chat with an old sailor, who afterwards became one of my best hands in the Bush, but the end was, that, in spite of my instinctive prejudice, I was drawn into intimacy with the mate. He could talk, and, like most persons who can, was communicative to a degree that he must have often found disagreeable, if not dangerous, but conversation was a necessity to him, and I have no doubt he would have related his adventures to a Black gin[5] or a Police officer, sooner than remain silent. So I used to sit smoking in the evening, and far on into the night, while he murmured away his adventures in his strong northern burr, like a talking mountain torrent.

I soon found that my companion was a finished scoundrel up to the chin, in every sort of rascality. On shore I should never have spoken to him twice: at sea he was amusing. He had been everywhere, and in every sort of craft, according to his own account; had had money and lived in great style, told stories of whales, slavers, Indiamen and pirates, by the dozen. He early confided to me that nothing but misfortune would have driven him to engage in such 'a miserable little tub of a craft, under such a know-nothing lubber as Captain Glum. A misfortune, Sir, that any gentleman might have fallen into.'

This misfortune, he presently let me know, consisted in having been convicted of bigamy and sentenced to two years' imprisonment. He had only been discharged a couple of days, when he joined us. To hear him, he was a victim,—just one of those heroic victims of London passions one meets with in French and German novels. He ended his story by saying,

'So I've paid the penalty; and now I'm free, and next time I shall manage better.' For already he had his eye on a third wife. After this, before turning in for that night, he begged a couple of shirts of me.

---

[5] Gin: native Australian name for an Aboriginal woman.

A few days afterwards he again drew me into conversation, saying,

'Excuse me, but I've been thinking what a pity it is that a smart, clever young gentleman like you, should go to bury yourself up in the Bush, beyond Sydney there. I've been up there myself, once; but there's no life, no fun, nothing suitable—nothing go-a-head, as the Yankees say. The sea's the thing for a man of spirit.'

'I thought there was very little to be done at sea, now-a-days.'

'No more there is in the old jog-trot;[6] but you have behaved very much like the gentleman, and I don't mind telling you a thing or two. I've been in a whaler hailing from Sydney; and it wasn't whales we made our money by, I can tell you. The time, it's about five years; we'd been out four months after sperm whale, and done next to nothing. I was second mate; the first mate was a Yankee, and the captain was a native Australian. The crew was a lot of all sorts and colours. One of our best harpooners was a New Zealander, and another a half-breed from Hudson's Bay. Some prime seamen among them, but not to be trusted ashore. Well there was a regular grumbling about our bad luck; for you see whalers are manned on the 'lay.' No wages, every man has a share in the take. I'd noticed the captain and the mate very thick, jawing together in a whisper up and down the quarter-deck; and so one day, it was a Sunday, mind, the captain slips into the cabin and soon after sends for me. There was he with the spirit-case before him, and the mate sitting cheek by jowl. 'Take a seat. A glass of grog, Mr. Clank;' says he, quite civil, and the mate gets up and shuts the door; 'help yourself;' and with that he shoves the rum over to me, 'and don't spoil it with water.' You may believe I didn't wait for twice asking; and it was prime stuff, surely; slipped down one's throat like new milk. 'Take another,' says he; and when he said that, I knew there was mischief up, let alone his being so civil. When I'd drawed my breath, the captain began again—

' "Bad luck so far, Mr. Clank; we shan't have much to take home for our wives and sweethearts, at this rate."

' "Why no," says I, "we couldn't have been more unlucky if we'd had a black cat or a parson aboard."

---

[6] Jog-trot: a regular jolting gait; a regular easy-going routine.

' "And yet," puts in the mate, "there's better things than whales to be found in these seas sometimes for those that have the pluck to pick them up!" I could see the captain was watching me all the time.

'So I answers, rather slow, "Well I'm game, as long as it's follow my leader." The captain gives a deep "*ah*," as if he was satisfied, and turning to the mate, with a wink, says, "Well I think we may put her about," and so he offered his box of Manillas[7] to take my choice, which I took for a hint to back out.

'That night we shifted our course until we got right into the Straits of Sunda.[8]

'One afternoon, a short time after this talk in the cabin, the mate calls to me, and puts his glass into my hand, and begs me to take a squint at something right aways[9] on our starboard bow.

' "What do you make out?" says he.

' "John Chinaman," says I, "a regular Noah's ark; one, two, three, a regular fleet of junks."

' "That's just it," says the mate, "these are better than sperm whales. That's the Monsoon fleet going down to buy goods at Singapore. There's a merchant in every one of those junks with a cabin like a parlour, a regular shop all to himself. He has his goods all nicely packed in small packages, and his money in silver ingots and dollars in jars ranged round like an apothecary's shop; so, as soon as it's dusk, I think we must go and do a bit of trade with the Chinaman."

'I dropped down in a minute. You know, Sir, I would not, on any account, have done anything against Christians like ourselves, but you see to take anything from these Pagans, with their Idols and their Joss Houses, was only spoiling the Egyptian—spoiling the Egyptian, Sir.'[10]

My squinting friend, who had been drinking all the time at my expense, said this with a sort of hypocritical snuffle, quite indescribable; perhaps he

---

[7] Manillas: cigars.

[8] Straits of Sunda: waters separating Java from Sumatra.

[9] Right aways: far away.

[10] 'Spoiling the Egyptians' (Exodus 13:35): spoils or booty of war taken from pagans.

was afraid of going too far with me. He continued, 'We kept edging off and on till it was dark, just keeping the junk fleet in view. I had a couple of boats all ready and some picked hands, a lot of cutlasses, and a dozen handspikes at the bottom of the boat under a sail. We said aloud we were going to have a trade with the Chinaman. The lights of the joss-houses served us to steer by; we did it as neat and comfortable as could be. The first junk the crew was all asleep until we were on deck, though it was a heavy climb, but we had hooks for that all ready.

'The mate knew where the merchant was to be found, walked straight there, while all but three kept guard forward, and in less than half an hour we had all the silver and half-a-dozen bundles of silk in the boats. The second junk we had to quilt[11] one fellow, though generally a dozen will run like sheep before one of our sort. Altogether we made a very good night of it, and before morning were clean out of sight; and we played that game as long as the season lasted. The crew were very well satisfied; we put into South American Ports, and got rid of the most knowing. When we got back into Sydney my share was better than three hundred pounds. I don't know what the captain said to the owners, but they seemed very well content to ask no questions.'

'Why, good heavens!' I involuntarily and foolishly exclaimed, at the end of this rascally relation, '… that was rank piracy.'

'Oh no, Sir, only not like cleaning out a square-rigged ship; those yellow pig-eyed fellows, with their pigtails, would not be believed on their oaths; only spoiling the Egyptians.'

So saying, he took a huge gulp at the grog. It was too dusk under the shadow of the sail for me to see the expression of his countenance, or for him to see that of mine, as he mouthed his pet phrase as if it had been an answer to everything.

Warming with the grog, and my silence, which he took for consent, he recommenced, 'Why, Sir, that's nothing to what a friend of mine did to get a cargo of sandal-wood. You see he was master of a small schooner in the sandal wood trade—that's a bartering trade with the South Sea Islanders,

[11] Quilt: (dialect) strike repeatedly; to thrash.

who are most of them fierce savages, and many of them cannibals. He'd sold his cargo pretty well and went into port to lay in a stock of articles for barter, and have a spree; and spree he did, to that extent that he not only spent all his money, but, when he came to be sober, he found he had married a lass that he certainly would not have chosen if he had known it; a regular vixen, above five feet ten, with a colour like a rose, and a lot of fair hair that hung to her waist nearly; a real beauty; but when her back was up, and that was about twice a day, she'd smash everything and everybody near. Well, here was a pretty concern, his money spent and a wife on his hands that would run him in more debt in a month than he could pay off in a year. However, it was done; he could not give up the port, it was too profitable; so he thought his case over calmly, and soon made up his mind.

'He invited his wife to go to sea for a short trip, which she was very willing to do. Before many weeks she'd given the captain a black eye and bred a mutiny. The men came aft and insisted on the lady being put ashore; however my friend managed to pacify them.

'At length they reached the Sandal Wood Island[12] and King Kettle came on board; an Indian king, so called because he had made a crown of a bright copper kettle. The captain presented him with a second-hand drummer's coat, besides other valuables, and introduced him to his wife, who divided the savage's admiration with the coat; he had never seen any white woman but an old one before.

'The captain went on shore with King Kettle, and the next day without the usual delays, the natives began bringing a cargo of sandal-wood down to the beach; they got the finest lot I ever saw; when it was loaded, King Kettle invited the captain and his lady to go ashore to a feast and dance. I will say that for her, she was afraid of nothing; the captain, before all the crew, recommends her not to go, and that makes her positive that she would. She puts on a light green satin dress with short sleeves, scarlet satin turban with

---

[12] Sandal Wood Island: now the Island of Sumba situated in the Indonesian Archipelago 400km east of Bali, and directly south of Komodo and Flores Islands. It contained vast quantities of native sandalwood and was populated by fierce warriors (per, *Sumba Foundation*).

an ostrich feather, all her hair hanging in curls down her back, and a pair of pocket pistols in her belt. She looked so grand, for all the crew were so mad with her goings on, they gave her three cheers when she stepped into the boat. Well, the captain came back alone, and told the crew his wife would stop, a piece of news that vexed nobody but one young fellow, who was for arming a boat, but nobody heeded him. At any rate, they up anchor and made sail, for it was a place where more than one ship's company had been murdered. However, there were people that will have it he sold his wife to King Kettle for that cargo of sandal-wood; and when, twelve months after, news came that King Kettle, after worshipping his white wife for some time, had had his patience exhausted like many others, and not only killed but eaten her, according to the custom of the country; my friend's only remark was an expression of wonder whether he digested her, "Because," says he, "if he did, King Kettle's the only person she ever could agree with!"

This story, so coolly told, quite finished me up. With a short good night and a very hollow laugh at King Kettle's digestion, I turned in, having first loaded my pistols and put them under my pillow. My dreams were not very pleasant. It would have been odd if they had been, transplanted so suddenly from the calm security of civilization to the middle of the ocean, bound up in the space of a few square feet, certainly without a friend, and probably with a felon.

I was awakened by a fearful cry, and rushed upon deck at the same time as the captain. There was a large ship bearing right down upon us, the man at the wheel in his fright threw the brig up into the wind.

'Starboard,' roared the captain to the stranger ship, snatching up a speaking trumpet, 'Starboard' we all shrieked in chorus, the shrill voice of the captain's wife above all. Through the moonlight I saw something white dash at the wheel of the stranger, and just as her bowsprit was over us she paid slowly off, and past us, grinding along our stern with a sound that chilled me to my heart. We were saved. The captain's wife fell on her knees and returned thanks for our wonderful escape; most of us followed her example, but when the mate, who had been lying in a drunken sleep on deck, came up rubbing his eyes, the captain snatched up a handspike[13] and knocked him down; the mate jumped and flew on him like a tiger, but the crew were too quick for him and got him down; in the mean time the captain had run for his pistols, but after a great row the mate went forward, and we all coiled down again in our berths.

A few days afterwards, the water turned bad. The owners, to save money, had given us half-cleansed beer-barrels, so it was decided to put into Rio de Janeiro. After the running-down night, the mate had been disrated, and sent forward among the men, for it was his watch, and it seemed as if the watches in both vessels had been asleep. From that time he was never sober. He had found out the way to bore a hole in a cask of rum, and suck at it through a thin bamboo tube every evening at dusk.

I was sitting one morning reading Don Quixote for the second time, when Clank came with a piece of wood in his hand, and asked me to lend him a large case-knife, that, among other foolish things stuck into emigrants, I had purchased for my outfit. I handed it to him without a word; he went straight to the grindstone and began to sharpen it. 'Halloa!' cried impudent little Duds, the cabin-boy, 'are you going to kill a pig this morning? A bit of fresh meat would be a treat.' 'You shall have fresh meat enough in five minutes,' was the answer. 'I'm going to cut that infernal captain's liver out!' and with that he sprang at the captain, who was just coming on deck. As luck would have it, one of the men, a sharp fellow, was coming aft, with a handspike. In an instant he threw it so cleverly, it took the mate between the legs and flung him flat; the knife flew out of his hand overboard, his head striking the captain in the middle of his fat paunch, upset him. Two or three of us jumped on top of the mate, who began to howl like a demon, and no wonder; for, in my anxiety to keep him down, I never thought of the cigar in my mouth, and all the time the crew were making a spread eagle of him, I was burning a hole in the back of his neck with the red end of it.

[13] Handspike: a wooden bar used as a lever.

We made him hard and fast, for he was raving mad with *delirium tremens.*[14] To cool him, every time the watch was called, the captain had a bucket or two of salt water thrown over him.

Four days before we reached Rio, a low, long, black schooner hailed and asked very anxiously for news from Europe. They sent a boat aboard us, and we all fully thought we were in for a regular clearance. The officer in command, a black-bearded, neat-looking little fellow, spoke broken English with a French accent. Whether it was that they were only slavers, or that we were not worth robbing, or that they had better business on hand; after accepting a file of newspapers, and asking me especially, as I spoke French, what news from France, they were about to depart, when the officer's eyes fell upon our prisoner in chains.

With a start, and a French oath, he exclaimed, 'T'ien c'est toi, Monsieur Louche, que diable fait-tu ici?'[15]

Then followed a whispering, which ended by the Frenchman coolly saying to the captain, 'Dis is a friend of mine; I vil save you de trouble of taking him any more.' With that they hurried into their boat, and in a few minutes we had seen the last of the Dominie,[16] as a Scotch sailor had named him.

Years passed before we met again.

---

[14] *Delirium Tremens* (D.T.'s): a violent delirium with tremors caused by alcohol withdrawal.

[15] (literally) 'Goodness, it's you, Monsieur Louche! What the devil are you doing here?'

[16] Dominie: schoolmaster (dialect Scotland).

6
Off to the Diggings!
John Capper

The *Jeremy Diddler*—a migrant ship.
Volume: 5 Number: 121 Pages: 405–10
Date: July 17, 1852
Fee: 5 pounds 10 shillings for 10 ½ Columns.

The future historian of the latter portion of this present nineteenth century will be called upon to decide whether June, 1851, or June, 1852, was the more exciting and interesting period. At Midsummer of the former year, Englishmen were rushing in tens of thousands to London to witness the great wonder of the day at Hyde Park. Midsummer of the present year is sending quite as many, and more, of our countrymen away from London—to say nothing of Liverpool and other places—as fast as sailing ships and steam-vessels can carry them, to join in the Golden Fair in Australia; the great South Land.

There has not been such an exodus from London within the recollection of the oldest ship-brokers; and they have, generally, pretty good memories, too. The only thing that is reported to me as at all coming up to it—though I don't believe it—was a general flight of elderly persons some fifty years since, when it was said that the earth was on the point of being burnt up by an exceedingly powerful description of comet.

Go where you will, everybody appears to be going 'off to the Diggings,' and everybody is in immediate want of outfits and passages. There are sixty young men rushing frantically away from their employers' counters in Saint Paul's Churchyard, and there are at least as many more longing to follow them. Fully five score of both sexes have bid adieu to Oxford Street and High

Holborn: and it is computed that quite one hundred and ten have migrated from the warehouses about Cheapside and Cripplegate. Then, there is the Old Lady of Threadneedle Street. She has furnished a respectable quota of clerks on eighty pounds a year, who are thirsting to handle the pick and the spade. I can't say how many youths at the Custom House and the Docks have drawn their last quarter's salary, and are now expending the amounts in Guernsey shirts, canvass trousers, American boots and wide-awakes. Legions of bankers' clerks, merchants' lads, embryo secretaries, and incipient cashiers; all going with the rush, and all possessing but faint and confused ideas of where they *are* going, or what they are going to do; beg of hard-hearted ship-brokers to grant them the favour of a berth in their last advertised teak-built, poop-decked, copper-bottomed, double-fastened, fast-sailing, surgeon-carrying emigrant ship.

Talk about the dreadfully depressed condition of the shipping interest, and the ruin of British ship-owners! I should like to find a man with whom to argue that point. I'd walk him down to the snug little crowded office of Messrs. Hopkins and Bung, ship-brokers, up one pair of stairs, in the City, and let him see the struggling, and elbowing, and beseeching for passages, going on there from ten in the morning until six in the evening, with two or three clerks taking down the names of applicants as fast as pens can write—and the pens at Hopkins and Bung's write uncommonly fast! There's no haggling or bickering about the price. Three words to a steerage passenger are all that the employers allow: intermediates are permitted half-a-dozen sentences, not one more.

There never were such times for speculative ship-owners and brokers. They haven't half enough vessels: to say nothing of crews to man them with. There's a huge bill with flaring letters against the office wall at Messrs. Hopkins and Bung's, that really looks quite imposing; and, certainly, if the unsuspecting crowd of emigrants who are spelling it, believe that more than half of the vessels named in it are anywhere within a hundred miles of the Docks in which they are said to be loading, it must be a very imposing list indeed. Why, one of those big-lettered ships was spoken off Land's End only yesterday; but I suppose the brokers have brought her up by the electric telegraph, for she is stated to be actually taking in cargo in the London

Docks. There's another vessel, with an enormously long East Indian name that none but the chief clerk can pronounce, which is believed to be not very far from the Chops of the Channel; yet she, too, by some broker's sleight-of-hand, is lying in the Docks, and will, positively, sail immediately after the *Jeremy Diddler*. However, it's 'all right' with the young men from Saint Paul's Churchyard and Cripplegate; their only idea of a voyage is an Easter excursion to Herne Bay and back; their sole acquaintance with sea-going dietary consists of unlimited orders to the steward for steaks, stout, and cigars. All day long, the names of eager, enthusiastic emigrants are posted in huge books that seem to be teak-built and copper-fastened like the ships; indeed, there are more passengers booked than any of the establishment know how to dispose of: the only chance of all being accommodated consisting in the possibility of some amongst them getting too ill to go, and, perhaps, a few falling overboard at Gravesend. It is dreadfully hard work, in the hot weather, at Hopkins and Bung's. The stoutest and youngest of their clerks are knocked up long before six o'clock, and the cashier is obliged to be taken home, every evening, in a cab.

It was a hot thundery day in the early part of June, when I bent my steps from the little office just named, towards the London Docks, along Fenchurch Street, down the Minories, and across Tower Hill, as fast as the dense throng would allow me. It appeared as if the best part of London, and a considerable portion of the Provinces, were going down on that particular day to engage berths for Australia. Every alternate shop seemed to have been suddenly converted into an outfitting warehouse. One man, more daring than his neighbours, actually offered the emigrating world complete outfits at forty-five shillings each, but whether it was for infants in arms or adults, I did not learn. Until that day I had but a very glimmering idea of the requirements of a gold-digger: on my way to the Docks, I learnt by the placards in the windows, that amongst the sundries needed at the 'Diggings,' were telescopes, alpaca umbrellas, reading-lamps, toasting-forks, easy-chairs, mirrors, and keybugles,[1] and many other miscellaneous articles.

[1] Keybugle: a bugle with six keys and a chromatic range of about two octaves.

The crowd became densely uncomfortable as I approached the Dock gates. The man in the Dock livery had given up the gate in despair: there was no such thing as keeping order. I found him, forlorn, in a remote corner, besieged by a crowd of intending emigrants, who were pressing him with a host of inquiries about the 'Diggings.' Whether they imagined him to have charge of all the shipping in the Docks, or whether they believed that the gold lace round his hat had been recently dug up at Mount Alexander, did not transpire, but it was quite evident that they felt confident in his knowing all about it; and when I left the spot, there was rather a strong party in favour of elevating the gatekeeper on the end of a rum-puncheon,[2] that all might catch his oracular words.

Through the defenceless gates, past some thousands of wine pipes that lay scattered about as though they didn't belong to anybody in particular, turning sharp round to the right along the water's edge, by the weighing sheds, where groaning, frowning, iron cranes, and bales of wool, and casks of tallow,[3] threatened the unwary passer-by;—and there, just before me, was the jetty.

What a sight there was upon that jetty! I could have fancied the whole export trade of the country had gone stark staring mad with the gold-fever, and had plunged out of bed and rushed down to the Docks. Boxes and cases, cart-wheels, hand-barrows, casks, and barrels, ploughs, crates, and bales, were all lying about in wild disorder, looking as though they would require a couple of years and a small army of labourers to stow them away. As to getting them all into the eight vessels—that I considered a matter of sheer impossibility, and not likely to be attempted.

On the right side of the jetty, midway down, lay the vessel I was in search of, the *Jeremy Diddler*, advertised 'for the Gold Regions, with immediate despatch,' and professing to be provided with an experienced surgeon, patent ventilators, family baths, and altogether the most superior accommodation of any ship or ships sailing from the port of London. A very few days previously,

---

[2] Puncheon: large cask of varying capacity.

[3] Tallow: rendered fat from cattle or sheep used to make soap, margarine, candles and lubricants.

the *Diddler* had been choked up with wool and tallow; at the moment of my visit, the sole vestiges of Australian produce in the *Jeremy Diddler* were the cockroaches, who were running all sorts of sweepstakes round the vessel, evidently quite at home.

About and around the ship, riggers, caulkers, smiths, carpenters, painters, were all working away, like so many steam engines, with a fifty-mechanic power that was quite invigorating to behold. Old men with grey hairs and faltering steps; young girls, pale from the factory or the garret; countrymen in smock-frocks; lean-faced artisans; mothers with infants in arms; stout servant girls; these and many others filed up the narrow, bending plank that formed a bridge between the old world and the new; and as I watched the motley troop pass on, I wondered much how some of those would fare in the wild gold-fields of the distant south.

There was no remaining on deck; not a soul appeared to care a straw about the masts, or the rigging, or the poop: the ship might have been without one or the other for aught they cared. All poured down to the ''tween decks,' by the little rickety wicked ladder that always pretended to slip about, yet never did: causing no end of little screams from under all sorts of bonnets.

The cool shade of the long range of 'tween decks seemed quite refreshing after the hot glare above. But, dear me, how crowded it was with candidates for emigration and sea-sickness! It was as much as the carpenters could do, to move their saws and chisels amidst all that myriad of limbs, without committing spontaneous amputation. I expected, more than once, to see several young children nailed down to the decks by their heels.

The entire length of the vessel had been cleared out, and was being marked off and divided into spaces for single, double, and treble cabins, as the wants of passengers might require. There were long lines, and curves, and zig-zags, chalked out on the decks under our feet, which might have been intended for a ground plan of the 'Maze' at Hampton Court, or the Catacombs at Paris. They were, in reality, sections of the embryo cabin accommodation; but whether intended to guide the work-people or to puzzle the visitor, was not clear. On one side, near the wicked ladder, an anxious group of emigrants were listening in breathless silence to the explanation given by a very young broker's clerk, in spectacles, as to the ground plan of the Maze. He pretended to make them understand where the port-holes would be cut through—one in each cabin; where the doors were to be placed; the precise spots where the sleeping-places and the tables would be found by and bye—with a variety of other matter, which might as well have been told in the Esquimaux[4] tongue. All listened with open mouths; and, when the young spectacles ceased and moved on to another group, they looked with a kind of hopeless credulity at each other.

In the stern of the ship, a numerous party had congregated round a little white deal coffin-like sort of a cabin—a model prison in miniature—run up in half-an-hour, just to show the passengers that the *Jeremy Diddler* was not going to do things like common ships. It was extremely amusing to see how anxiously and curiously the many visitors were scrutinising that wretched packing-case. I could imagine them to have been admiring and gloating over the suite of Austrian apartments in the Great Exhibition. To be sure, the fittings set off the thing rather smartly; but, I don't remember seeing any cabin of that same size in the *Diddler*, when I visited her afterwards; and certainly none with such polished chairs, drawers, and wash-stand; nor, with such exquisite white bedding in them. The effect of this one cabin was perfectly marvellous. There seemed to be something magical about the very wood-work: the door was moved to and fro as if it were expected to play tunes on its hinges; the brass hooks were eyed by more than one with a view to see if they were not of real Australian gold. As for the swing-tray, I am sure several young women believed it to be some sort of cot for an infant; while others gazed on the little neat shelves, the sly drawers under the bed, the hanging lamp, and the sea-chest, as reverently and cautiously as if they had all been dangerous tricks in a pantomime, chock full of secret springs and sudden transformations.

It was easy to see that of the whole crowd of uninitiated subjects of Her Majesty, very few indeed, if any, descended the narrow plank to the jetty, with a more approximate idea of how they were to be cabined and dieted, than when they left their homes in the morning. All they could have

---

[4] Esquimaux or Esquimau: Eskimo (Fr.).

dreamed of that night would be a confused jumble of crooked chalk-lines, port-holes, swing-trays, and bulk-heads; but, whether they had to go through the port-holes to their beds, or whether they would dine upon the swing-trays, or whether the bulk-heads had any bodies or limbs attached to them, would be far beyond their comprehension. I could scarcely believe my senses, when I read in a morning paper some twelve days or so after my visit to the Docks, a notice to passengers by the *Jeremy Diddler*, informing them that they must be prepared to join that vessel at Gravesend on the following day. Having satisfied myself that there was really no mistake about the thing, but

Figure 5.2 Tea Water, Scenes on board migrant ship with a horse shown standing in its stall while tea water is distributed. *Illustrated London News*, 20 January 1849.

that she would positively anchor off the town of Gravesend at the time named, I prepared to take my departure by steamer, in order that I might see the last of her and her human cargo on this side the blue waters.

The same boat which conveyed me from Blackwall carried several parties, evidently to the same destination. There were two or three newly wedded couples, brought together, doubtless, on the strength of future 'Diggings;' a knot of oily-headed, sleek-visaged shopmen, and City clerks; a few hale-looking country lads and lasses; and a rather extensive family of nondescripts; all of whom, by their conversation, were passengers for the *Jeremy Diddler*. The morning had been what nautical men term 'breezy,' and when we reached the Terrace Pier at Gravesend, the wind had become quite violent in its proceedings, committing assaults of an outrageous description on the dresses of the lady passengers; so much so, that the police of the Corporation might very well have interfered and indicted it before the mayor for disorderly and riotous conduct. As for the shipping at anchor off the town, it was, evidently, but little better: some of the outward-bounders had no doubt been taking a parting glass with the old Custom-house hulk off the Ordnance wharf, and were rather the worse for it. They were rolling, and staggering, and bobbing about, winking their port-holes at each other, and flirting their blue-peters[5] in the air, in a way that no respectable, steady-going vessels would think of doing. It was quite clear, that one or two among them meant to make a night of it, from the determined way in which they kicked up their keels, and splashed the water over decent wherries[6] and passengers-boats.

I was rather glad to scramble up the black and white sides of the *Diddler*, out of the overloaded boat, where the young married women were screaming as they were being packed by twos in a cask and hauled up, while the oily-headed shopmen looked in dismay at the rope-ladder over the side, and wished in their hearts they were females, for the sake of the tub and pulley.

---

[5] Blue-peter: a blue signal flag with a white square in the centre used to indicate that a merchantman was about to sail.

[6] Wherry: a long light row boat with a pointed end used to transport passengers on rivers and harbours.

Well, there I was, once more, on the deck of this very fast-sailing, clipper-built,[7] copper-fastened, passenger ship, bound to the Gold Regions, by the advertisement in the *Times*—but, I should have thought, sailing to Botany Bay, by the dismal misery written on the faces of those on deck! Transportation for life, with stone-breaking in heavy chains, appeared distinctly visible in their countenances. Some were trying to look unconcerned, and even rather jolly, as if they knew all about it, and it was a mere nothing to them; others got up a little careless whistling, and put questions to the pilot in an imitative gruff voice; some reeled and staggered from the hatchway to the scuppers[8] like drunken men, while others held on with a gripe of despair by the spare anchor under the long-boat, as if expecting the ship to founder, and they meant to make a life-buoy of *that*. None were actually ill, but there was, scattered about, every stage of incipient sea-sickness.

I made my way to the main-hatch, and began to descend the ladder. 'On deck there!' cried a voice below that seemed to come up from the farthest corner of a very deep cask. 'Ay, ay!' growled the sailor addressed, who was busily engaged in some mysterious operation with the long-boat. 'Where have you stowed your patent ventilators?' inquired the voice from the cask, 'we're choking down here.' 'Oh,' rejoined the tar, as he winked at the cook's mate, 'Neptune will bring them there a-board when he visits us at the Line!'

The complaint was indeed well founded, as I felt on descending into the regions below, where I found the man with the casky voice. The complainant was a middle-aged person, a tailor or shoemaker perhaps, disguised as a naval character according to the most approved fashion at the Surrey Theatre. It took me some minutes before I could distinguish the lights and shades of the living panorama moving in that long, half-obscure vault of a place. How changed since I saw it in the Docks! The uproar, the crowd, the handing about of packages and clothing, the dim indistinct light from the far

---

[7] Clipper-built (like a clipper ship): a fast sailing ship especially developed by American builders around 1840: having long slender lines, tall raking mast and large sail area.

[8] Scuppers: an opening in the sides of a ship for draining water from the deck.

distant fore-hatch, gave it the appearance of Rag Fair held in the Thames Tunnel for novelty's sake.

There was small room for walking about. I had to clamber over all sorts of sharp-cornered, hard-edged packages. Children were crying, women were chattering, men were grumbling and swearing, and calling down the ugliest maledictions upon the heads of all the captains, chief-mates, brokers, and ship-owners in the known world. On the whole, it was confusing to a new-comer, and not much plainer, apparently, to those who had been on board during the last twenty-four hours. Had the captain poured the entire contents of the London Dock warehouse down an enormous funnel into that particular 'tween decks, the chaos could scarcely have been aggravated. The staggering motion of the vessel set all landsmen's attempts to labour at complete defiance. As for the women, they were content to seat themselves on anything that was nearest their cabins, and there contemplate the encompassing wilderness of property.

There were a few exceptions in the way of work, and these at once attracted my attention. Adjoining the main-hatch, there was a family scene presenting a strong and interesting contrast to the angry idleness around. The mother had placed three young children securely on the deck, between boxes lashed down so that they could not move, and there they played together contentedly, while she busied herself with arranging the little clean bed-linen as tidily as a head chambermaid at a first-class hotel. She had made up her orderly mind that there was not to be such a thing as a crease in the pillow-case; and, as for the snow-white sheets, she seemed to expect some of the nobility to sleep in them—if you could have fancied any nobility, however old, being of greater importance to her, at that moment, than her own plebeian family. The husband was not less busily engaged in securing their various little cabin comforts; although these appeared to be few enough. He seemed to know how to make the most of them, though; and was bent upon not giving in until he had accomplished his task.

It was quite a relief to watch that energetic persevering man and his bustling wife, after seeing so much discomfort about the decks. He evidently prided himself upon the perfect manner in which he had fastened up a few little pewter drinking mugs at the side of the cabin, out of all fear of knocking their heads against the handles. Few men on board could have accomplished that feat. Then there was a long strip of leather nailed up at intervals, in which spoons, forks, combs, and brushes were inserted, bidding stern defiance to the heaviest lurches of the ship. The little square looking-glass, however, was his *chef d'œuvre,*[9] he had secured it by nails and white tape, and there was not the least fear of its giving way. He was not quite sure, though, that it was in the centre, and retreating from the cabin until he fell over a whole waggon-load of goods, he took an elaborate survey of its position. He looked at it from all sorts of distances and points; he peeped through both eyes and then through only one; he gazed attentively from the summit of a sea-chest, and then tried the effect of it from one of the opposite cabins. This man's destiny I saw at a glance. His fortune is as good as made. I shouldn't object to share in his future prosperity; for it will be steady and lasting, and more ample than that of many an emigrant who takes out a lump of capital to work upon. This family are all excellent, from the tips of their hair to the soles of their feet; there's nothing worthless about them.

How different the party of men and women I saw near them, half-washed, half-clad, half boisterous, half drowsy. The men were trying to get up a game with a dirty pack of cards, but it was scarcely possible to see the marks on them. A short distance from my industrious friends was another family group not less interesting. A grey-haired old patriarch was nursing an infant to sleep in his feeble arms, while a young woman prepared its little bed. There seemed to be no other person of their party; their cabin was but poorly furnished, and in her thin sorrowful face and the old man's stricken form, I thought I could read their little history of sorrow and suffering. They were not going to the Diggings to escape from the scenes of the past; a new life in a new world was her sole object, and the old father cared for nothing but to accompany her.

In one densely packed cabin I saw the fragments of several families busily engaged in quarrelling about their respective shares of space. How they intended to stow a tithe of the lumber scattered and piled about, I was at a loss to imagine. Somebody had knocked the cork out of a bottle of ink, the

---

[9] *Chef d'œuvre*: chief or master work (Fr.).

contents of which had flowed in sable streams over bed-clothing, towelling, and children's dresses, indelibly marking them in the wrong places. Next to these noisy malcontents were a party of four females, two of whom were rather advanced in years, and stout withal. There were great lamentations proceeding from these ladies, who had evidently some deep distress weighing upon their minds. As I halted near their cabin door, one of the heavy females was seeking the advice and consolation of a fellow passenger, in their difficulty; which appeared to consist in the dreaded impossibility of their being able to get into one of the beds. The lower sleeping-place was all right; one stout lady would blend with a thin one beautifully, though there would be no width to spare; but how and by what imaginary contrivance the other stout lady was to arrive at her destination for the night, seemed to them a matter of the wildest speculation. The cabin was too low for a ladder, and the berth was too high for a box or a folding-stool to be of the least service beyond aggravating the temper, and perhaps bruising a few limbs.

Passing forward to near the fore-hatchway, I came upon a scene of open war. One of the ship's officers was endeavouring to read a sort of impromptu riot-act to a party of cockney warriors who were doing all sorts of violent deeds in a dark smothered up cabin, which was evidently in a state of determined siege. The lookers-on cried, 'Shame! Turn them out!—where's the captain?' mingled with rather warm benedictions on the ship's broker, and the secretary of some emigration committee. The officer would have interfered, but the bystanders opposed him, and it ended in his disappearing on deck, and the siege of the darkened little cabin being raised. I learnt afterwards, when quiet was partly restored, that the *fracas* arose from the brokers having shipped more passengers than could be accommodated; a dozen persons had been, two days before, removed from the ship by the emigration officers; but in their place at least a score more had been sent on board, and where they were to find room was now the question. The captain had been trying to place two men in some single berths.

But this, I ascertained, was not all of the mismanagement, or imposition, or both, from which these unfortunate emigrants suffered. A great number of them had paid for their passages through some emigration society, which had secured room for them in the bulk, at a stated sum. Now, however, at the twelfth hour, these poor people were told that the brokers had demanded two pounds a head more from the society, owing, it was stated, to the rise in sailors' wages; and they accordingly found themselves called upon to make good the amount from their scanty purses. It was not [to] be wondered at, therefore, that there should be a considerable amount of angry feeling amongst the three hundred and odd emigrants on board the *Jeremy Diddler*. Neither was it matter for surprise that fault was found with the cook for being too idle to clean his soup coppers out, and allowing an accumulation of filthy, rank dirt around them, to the actual spoiling of what might have been very respectable soup.

By way of interlude to the recent siege, an emigrant orator mounted on a sea-chest, as well as the pitching of the ship would allow him, and addressing his fellow passengers in terms of brotherly commiseration, which might have suited Marc Anthony's oration to the Romans, he drew a heart-rending picture of their distresses, not omitting the dirty soup and the absence of the patent ventilators spoken of in such large letters in the broker's bills. The speaker was the man with the casky voice and the Surrey nautical.[10] How long he would have held forth I cannot undertake to surmise, for his eloquence was brought to a sudden close by the heavy fall of the fore-hatch, which enclosed us all in utter darkness. The rain was beginning to pour, and the deck strollers crept down as well as they could.

The close, stifled atmosphere of the 'tween decks, breathed as it was by several hundred persons, soon became insupportable, and there was a general attack made upon the hatch, which, however, was too well secured above to allow of any success. The tide of indignation vented itself upon the main-hatch, through which a party of a dozen passed to the captain with expostulation as to the want of fresh air. After some delay, the fore-hatch was partially removed, and an old tattered windsail[11] was let down as a substitute for the patent ventilators. In spite of this relief, the impurity and suffocating

---

[10] Surrey nauticals: to be dressed in the style of a naval character at the Surrey Theatre.

[11] Windsail: a wide tube or funnel of canvas used to carry air for ventilation into the lower compartments of a ship.

heat of the cabins became as insupportable as the exhalations from some Indian jungle-swamp; and I could but picture to myself the sufferings of those people when approaching the equator.

The cabins were built up, two deep, on both sides, and made to contain never less than two sleeping places; often four. To reach the inner cabins the passengers had to grope their way along a narrow dark passage between the outside cabins; and inasmuch as not more than every alternate one enjoyed the luxury of a small round port-hole, the close heated feel within them may be imagined. I looked for the neat, roomy model cabin with its many fittings, that had attracted so much notice when I visited the ship in dock; but my search was in vain. It had gone the way of all models, or was perhaps doing duty on board the next vessel on the berth, together with the patent ventilators and the family baths.

It was some time past twilight when I left the ship's side, having taken a parting peep at the emigrant Babel below; and, with the sound of the casky voice still ringing in my ears, complaining bitterly of some newly discovered mine of grievances, I bade my boatmen pull ashore. Early the following morning I strolled down to the Town Pier, and reached it in time to see the *Jeremy Diddler* steamtugged round the point of land below. My immediate reflections were, that I very much approved of emigration, and that it was very natural and reasonable in large numbers of our home-community, who have little or no prospect of ever establishing themselves in life on their own account, here, to go with a good spade and as good a will, to the Diggings, But, also, that the *Jeremy Diddler*, and the subject of passenger accommodation in general, would be none the worse for a little more 'ventilation.'

7
Post to Australia[1]

Edward Michael Whitty

Steamship services to Australia were being disrupted because of the Crimean War.
Volume: 13 Number: 316 Pages: 305–06
Date: April 12, 1856
Fee: 2 pounds 2 shillings for 3 Columns.

The firm that I am connected with does not believe in letters: their faith is in personal interviews. They do not write about business: they transact it. The consequence is, that I am always at sea: I am always going between Austinfriars and Australia. Not being brought up to the sea, it cannot be expected that I should like this.

I am not a scientific man. I have never even been to the Polytechnic Institution. But, not having anything particular to do at sea besides to be sick, I indulge in attempts to invent methods of facilitating the delivery of persons and letters between St. Martin's-le-Grand, London, and Broad Street, Melbourne, in spite of the chaplain of the clipper Presto, in which I have just arrived; who considers that it is an impiety to be interfering with Nature's geography. He says that the world was made round, and that we ought to go round it in the regular manner, when we want to go from one place to

---

[1] See also, 'The Great Screw', (*Household Words*, 22 October 1853, No. 187, pp. 181–84; see also p. 18 in this volume) which describes the effects of steam shipping on global communications, including mail deliveries. See also, 'Short Cuts across the Globe' (*Household Words*, 13 April 1850, No. 3, pp. 65–68; see also p. 6 in this volume) about shipping and the need for the Panama Canal to be built.

another. But I take the commercial ground; and,—observing that a general re-arrangement of the world seems going on: that the Nicaraguan Canal is being made a short cut across America, and the Suez Canal is to give the go-by to the Cape of Good Hope—I don't see why I should not have my scheme for getting to Australia.

It may startle at first—I admit that it is bold—but the late Mr. George Stephenson remarked before a parliamentary committee, that the making a railway to the moon was merely a question of expense; and Australia is not the moon. On the contrary, Australia is the antipodes. That very phrase suggests my scheme. Instead of going round to Australia, why not go down to Australia? An Artesian well is merely a matter of cost. If it costs so much to make an Artesian well two miles deep, of course it can only cost so much more to go on making it right through the earth. I don't mean to say that if you bored straight down, you would come out precisely at Melbourne; but you could tunnel in that direction. You could worm your way down. It would take time and money; but I suppose the Appian Way took time and money, and M. de Montalembert[2] suggests that we are very like the Romans. We should more than justify the comparison, if we could drop our letters and newspapers down a tube to Australia. To me, personally, it would be a great convenience to be let down in that way; for our firm, in establishing branches at Sydney and Melbourne, *will* have personal interviews; and I am the only man, they tell me, that they can trust.

Something must be done. The more the colonies develop themselves, the harder it is to get at them. Our firm says, that it is all the fault of the Lords of the Treasury. My Lords cannot, naturally, be expected to take much interest in commercial questions. But, if the principle, suggested by the chaplain of the Presto, that you should be made to go round the earth, be a Conservative principle, it is a Liberal principle, I should think, that you may go across the earth, and that is what the present Lords of the Treasury in a Liberal government strictly forbid. They will make you take the longest way, and

---

[2] Marc René de Motalembert (1714–1800): French military engineer and technical writer, known as the architect of modern fortifications. He also wrote stories and verse and for some time lived in England.

resort to the slowest means of taking the longest way. Consequently, our firm is not very successful with the branches at Sydney and Melbourne. Our firm—and the fact is true also of the whole trade of England—exports more goods to Australia than to any other part of the globe, the United States excepted. Australia is deemed the best market we now have in the world. Our firm—and that is also true of the Bank of England—has been saved from a commercial crisis this past year's winter by the gold I and others have brought home from the Diggings. Our firm has lost, in the interest on money floated round the world, in compliance with the views of my Lords, a sum which would enable the senior partner to retire, comfortably. The total sum lost in interest by the entire commercial community would make my tube. I have calculated it carefully at per vertical mile. Well, then, I say something ought to be done.

When I first began to go to Australia, in eighteen hundred and fifty-two, it was not so bad. You could go by screw-ships, viâ the Cape. To be sure, they all broke down, or went ashore, or never got to Melbourne; and our firm told the authorities that they would break down, or go ashore, and never get there. But it was an experiment and it showed attention on the part of the Lords of the Treasury. You could also go—and that was the way our firm sent me—by the Peninsular and Oriental Company's route. It was zig-zag, which is nearly as bad as all round about; but it was fast. You rushed to Marseilles, and caught a boat there. You rushed across the Isthmus of Suez, and caught a boat there. You got to Point de Galle,[3] and caught a boat there; and, if you were lucky in hitting the boats, you got to Melbourne in about seven weeks after leaving London. The boats between Point de Galle and Melbourne were nothing to speak of. They were little, and overcrowded, and dirty, and slow; but, then, it was only a colony that you were going to, and the Peninsular and Oriental Company, having taken the contract at a low rate in order to keep rivals out of their waters, were not likely to ruin their shareholders. But what happened? When the war broke out, our firm said to me, 'We must make new arrangements with our branch at Sydney; you must be off there to-night.'

[3] Point de Galle: modern city of Galle in Sri Lanka.

I went to the Peninsular and Oriental Company, and asked about the berths from Point de Galle. 'Dropped that service,' said the clerk. No boat from Point de Galle! The fact is, the Peninsular and Oriental had given up several of their boats to the Government for the conveyance of troops to the Crimea; and they had convinced the Lords of the Treasury that the Point de Galle screws must stop running. Just then, our firm was doing a tremendous business with Australia; yet my Lords managed to keep up steam postal service to India, Brazil, Spain, West Indies; places that did not take one-sixth part of the value of the goods that were pouring into Australia: but they left Australia nearly destitute. Our firm and several other firms remonstrated, but my Lords had made up their minds; and, during the seventeen months that have elapsed since the Peninsular and Oriental got off their Point de Galle contract, I and others have had to go round the world, and to go in sailing ships. Capital clippers, the Liverpool clippers, but they take eighty to one hundred days in going, and not very much less in coming. Now, why, as a colony increases, should you diminish the facilities of getting to it, the war notwithstanding? I would be much obliged if my Lords would answer that.

But my Lords are going to do something, now that there is Peace. They have issued a minute, in which they are good enough to tell us commercial men, that there are three ways of getting to Australia; viâ the Cape; viâ Suez; and viâ Panama; and—with great modesty, declining to pronounce any opinion of their own, as to which is best—they ask the six Australian colonies to consider and agree which route shall be adopted. They invite steam-ship companies to tender for all the routes. This is no doubt believed to be very energetic; but, all the while that the six colonies are wrangling—as they are sure to do—I shall still have to go by the clippers; for it will be at least a year before anything can be settled. Our firm says, 'Put on the Point de Galle boats again.' But the Lords of the Treasury are not going to prejudge the question in that way. Other firms say, that if the Official Hydrographer (a person who would rather puzzle you in an argument, I should think) be set to calculate, he would very soon find out which is the shortest route—commercial men generally regarding the shortest route as the best route. They say, that if you draw a line from London to Melbourne it will go by

Dover, Paris, Marseilles, Suez, the Chagos Islands,[4] across the Indian Ocean, right into Broad Street, Melbourne; that there are railways, steamers, and caravans into Suez: and that all that has to be done is to put ten-knot steamers on between Suez and Melbourne. This would land letters between London and Melbourne in forty-four days. But my Lords say, that although this is very true, the form must be gone through of waiting a year or so until the colonies have fought out the battle of routes.

I say—Make the tube; or, if you will not go to that expense, cut as straight across the globe as you can; and, for mercy's sake, get the circumnavigating discussion out of the Circumlocution Office as fast as possible.

[4] Chagos Archipelago: in the Indian Ocean 500km south of the Maldives.

8
We Mariners of England
Samuel Rinder and Henry Morley

Grievances of merchant seamen regarding working conditions; and the need for the government to legislate and implement changes to protect their welfare. Some references to Australia.
Volume: 6 Number: 153 Pages: 553–57
Date: February 26, 1853
Fee: 3 pounds for 8 ¼ Columns.

I and my shipmates have more things to growl about than our bad lodging in the forecastle. Ashore I'm not much given to grumbling; Dorothy knows and can bear witness (Dorothy does know and bears witness) that I'm not a grampus.[1] But I bear my part afloat when we talk ship matters over, and if owners and Members of Parliament really want to know why sailors run the English merchant service, the forecastle is the place they ought to come to for their information. Maybe we're wrong in some of our notions, not being learned men: and when I plot with Dorothy to get somebody to print a little of the common seaman's mind for us, I don't want my words to be taken as a statement of what is wrong about us; what I'm going to say only concerns what we think wrong, when, in our unlearned way, we talk the matter through between ourselves.

There's an act, I believe, called the New Navigation Act, to regulate the manning of merchant ships; we get told about it sometimes, but it don't answer its purpose. When a ship is undermanned or manned with half

[1] Grampus: a person who breathes heavily and loudly.

tailors and shoemakers, and most of *them* skulkers,[2] the seaman is worked harder, I can tell you, than he ought to be. It is not very long since the first and second officers of the Indiaman Alfred were charged at the Thames Police Office with deserting their ship at Portsmouth. They ran the ship because they found out, after sailing, that the crew was made up of old men, boys, and lubbers who had been picked up great bargains. They took three hours to reef the ship's top-sails off Hastings.

The American owners know the value of an able sailor, and they pay the price for him, and make him lie contented in his berth, because it *is* a berth and not a dog-hole. Whenever an American clipper runs over to England with a freight from India or China, she comes partly manned with Malays, Lascars,[3] and South Sea Islanders. Such seamen she discharges in London or Liverpool, and fills their places up with English ablebodied salts. Our men are so eager to get aboard American vessels, that they pay premiums of a pound and thirty shillings to the men who get them berths. The coloured men sent adrift from the American ships are, many of them, hired at small pay by the English owners, and the rest are thrown upon the streets as vagrants or crossing-sweepers.

I don't know whether a bill has not been passed lately—by honourable gentlemen who know more of the grievances talked of in the cabin than of the grievances we grumble over in the forecastle—for the apprehension of deserters. Reciprocal treaties, I think they call them, were to be made with Russia, Sweden, Peru and any other states that would consent, for the giving up seamen like so many thieves and blackguards if they left their vessels. To be sure, under some Act good for owners, there is a contract signed, the effect of which is in most cases that we may be dismissed at any port; but never may dismiss ourselves within the term for which we sell our bodies to the owner. Ships' articles and shipping-masters seem to us to be made always taut one way and loose another. Articles often are set down off-hand in this way, for 'A voyage from the port of (say) Plymouth, to such place as the masters may direct, for a period *not exceeding* two years.' We may be

[2] Skulker: a person who skulks–to avoid work or responsibility; to shirk; malinger.

[3] Lascar: East-Indian sailor.

discharged at any time within two years and always at any place. We may be turned loose on the coast of Guinea; but we must never go loose of our own will. Emigrant ships are looked after, and must be seaworthy; but merchant vessels may be sent out, if the owner likes, without a bottom. Sink or swim, we must go with the hull: we are a part of it. It is not long ago that, at Liverpool, the seamen of the *Seringapatam*, knowing her to be unseaworthy, refused to go out in her, and went to jail instead. The ship sailed and on the second day put back, too leaky to go any further. But the seamen had, meanwhile, been sent to jail, because, though they were right, it wasn't their opinion the law cared about. The law was made for owners, not for such as them. That's our notion on the subject.

It makes us laugh, as we eat chalky biscuit in our dark hole of a forecastle, to hear about all this pious horror of desertion, and about sending ships of war to Australia and Quebec to prevent it; as if it was ships of war that the men wanted. The Americans pay seamen ten pounds a month for the voyage to California; while owners in London are allowing landsmen to work out their passage to Australia at five pounds a head, and enter such men as a portion of the crew. As if this didn't pinch us sailors, that do know something about seamanship, sharply enough, we are sent out with two pound ten a month, and sometimes no advance and never an allowance made to wives or parents. Those wages are given although freights have advanced thirty per cent., and men hired in Australia for England would not work a ship for twice the money. Of course, when we have got out to Australia, we very often don't choose to come home upon such terms.

A Queen's ship is to be sent, I've heard, to the St. Lawrence to try and stop desertion at Quebec. Labour lost, I'll wager! Why, the worst craft that sail upon water are the hulks that go out to Quebec for timber. The men are knocked up with extra labour, working at the pumps. The vessels are neither coppered nor sheathed; and, on the return voyage, all sorts of plans are contrived to keep some of them from tumbling asunder in the sea. The *Venus* brig came home with as many as seven chains passed under her, to bind her frame together. Then they sail badly—as may be supposed—make long voyages, and run short of provisions. The logs of timber, on the return voyage, are piled high above the long-boat, and washed about the deck by the sea. It is no wonder that the crews of such craft will desert, when seamen can earn a dollar a day in the country dragging timber; and when crimps are offering them all kinds of inducements from the builders of new ships, and the masters of vessels bound to port for want of hands. As for stopping the crimps[4] from taking us in tow by orders from the holystoned[5] deck of a man-of-war,[6] I should like to see anybody stopping them. There is nowhere a stricter river police than at Quebec. The men row round about the ships armed to the teeth; they are up to every move; and, what is more, know all the crimps, but still the work goes on at a rare rate in spite of them.

It is all very well to have shipping-masters appointed by the owners to act between us, give us contracts to sign, to pay us and to take our receipts. We do not like the shipping-masters, for we see that they take more pains to secure us to the owners than to see that we have been considered fairly. 'Tis a pity that we are not better at our learning. I knew a man, James Glandford is his true name, seaman of the Rodney, who found out when he took the balance of his wages at the shipping-master's office, after a voyage to Hobart Town and Ceylon, that he had made a blunder, and had been underpaid three pounds. But he had given a release, and could not get the mistake set right again, either by force or favour. If the shipping-master would have helped him to make out his small bit of adding and subtracting, he would have had his dues. But that wasn't the shipping-master's business. He did not represent the forecastle interest.

But of all schemes put in force against us that we are told to consider for our good, there is none discussed more than what is called the Registration Act. There is one owners' clause in it that we think rather insulting. It is that in case of wreck or loss of ship, every surviving seaman shall be entitled to his wages only on the production of a certificate from the master or chief

---

[4] Crimps: persons who get men to serve as sailors and soldiers by force or trickery.

[5] Holystone: a large flat piece of sandstone used by seamen for cleaning the deck of a ship–so called as it was used on Sunday.

[6] Man-of-war: an armed naval vessel; a warship.

Figure 5.3 Deck of the *Union of London*, 1823. *Jack Tar: a Sailor's Life 1750–1910*, Woodbridge: Antique Collectors' Club, 1999.

surviving officer, to say that he 'exerted himself to the utmost to save ship, cargo and stores.' It is to be assumed that he didn't do his duty, unless somebody will step forward and vouch for him that he did. If the clause had said that seamen having been proved guilty of neglect of duty in the hour of shipwreck should forfeit their wages, that would have been another thing, and not offensive to us. As it is, though, it is better for those by whom such clauses are suggested, no doubt. It leaves owners a better chance of saving something from the wreck, though it be saved out of a survivor's wages. I don't say that I think—because I do *not* think—that there are many owners who would use any ungenerous construction of this clause; but there the clause is, and we think it shows the spirit of the law, hauling taut against the forecastle, but all a-slack in favour of the owners and the after-cabin.

But the great fact about the Registration Act is that, according to it, we are all ticketed and numbered; and without producing his ticket a man cannot be admitted to employment under the English flag. That is no grievance, to be sure; we go and sail under the stripes and stars. To us sailors these documents are so much lumber; they are of no use to us in the world. We must produce them here, produce them there, and Jack has to go before a magistrate if he should lose his ticket. Then he gets another and pays a fine of from two to ten shillings and costs. The consequence of all this registering and passporting is, that when a man has once deserted, he deserts for good and all. If he's to be identified and put in prison or fined wages when he gets to England, he takes good care to remain with brother Jonathan. The system costs, I think, somewhere about ten thousand a year, but the big register of all our names and ages can take no account of those who work their passage to America, nor of those that ship aboard Yankee vessels in England; and loses sight of those that quit seafaring life and settle down ashore, and of those that die in the colonies, or emigrate; and can't take note of any of the odd drains that have carried men away for seventeen years—to say nothing of our being scattered and living and dying unheard of by the Registrar in all parts of the world. So I hope the list will be found important to the nation on the breaking out of war. However the Register, such as it is, mayhap is better than no register at all, and I take it for granted that there are reasons for all these things that a gentleman from Parliament could show to us, just as we could show to him, what manner of life we lead; and not to be too bold in finding fault with legislation, I will just make an end of what I want to say by giving a short account of how we work on board a merchant vessel, having shown already how we eat and sleep and lodge.

From daylight to dark we are all busily employed. The sails, spars, and rigging are always being overhauled and made right, as we sail from port to port; in fine weather not an idle minute is permitted. We count our time, as landsmen know, by bells, one bell being half-an-hour. Each twenty-four hours contains seven watches; five watches of four hours, or eight bells each, and two dog-watches, of two hours or four bells. These last come between four and eight o'clock of afternoons. The crew is then divided into two equal sets, called the starboard and the larboard watch. The starboard watch is under the orders of the captain and second mate, the larboard watch under the first mate and perhaps a third mate or a boatswain. Those are the men, and those are the hours, and the supposition is that the two sets of men relieve each other every four hours, except during the dog-watches, when they shift their order, to the end that the same men may not always have the same watches to keep. That is the supposition, which allows for every man on board the vessel twelve hours of work on deck, and twelve hours for rest, food, and sleep below. In practice we have nothing of the sort; ships must be well manned that can afford to be content with twelve hours a day of work out of the sailor. The afternoon watch, from noon until four o'clock, and the first dog-watch, from four to six, are kept by all hands, except in very rough weather. The consequence of this is, that the men who have stood the middle night-watch from midnight until four in the morning, turn in for four hours, and at eight o'clock must be on deck again to take their turn from eight to twelve; but after twelve all hands are kept on deck till six, so that the men who have kept the middle night-watch work all day from eight to six, except only by an hour allowed them for their dinner. At six o'clock they get short rest, because the rotation being changed, they turn in only for the dog-watch until eight, and then must come on deck to go on keeping watch till midnight. Thus each half of the crew takes turn with a day of extra labour, in which there are eighteen hours of duty and six hours of rest, those hours of rest not being in one heap but in two separate portions, one of four and one of two hours only. Even these snatches of sleep are liable to be interrupted by a sudden rise of wind, and that unwelcome cry that it blows to us: 'All ha-a-ands reef topsails! Tumble up, there! tumble up!'

In the succeeding twenty-four hours, the men that have been overworked get twelve hours on deck and twelve below. The average rest allowed to the sailor is therefore about nine hours a day, in which he must get through his sleep, meals, washing, clothes-mending, and other necessary occupations. This allowance would be little enough if it were given in a lump; but it is made more insufficient of course when it is cut up into slices, which, of necessity, are again subject to so many interruptions and deductions. In nearly all ships, American as well as English, this division of time and labour is adopted. It wears us out; it uses us up too fast; and many an accident that has resulted from a drowsy look-out, or a discontented crew, may make it doubtful whether the plan is always, so much as it appears to be, a source of gain to the owner on each voyage. Some masters refuse to their hands even the forenoon watch below, and keep the men on deck twenty hours one day, and fourteen hours the next. If any forecastle man could get into Parliament from one of these All Hands Crafts, I reckon he would bring them in a sweeping Ten Hours Bill. Sea air has need to be wholesome. There is little else good for the health of a sailor in an English trading ship.

I never saw any other system of work followed on board ship, except once when I was in a Sydney whaler, and we formed a plan of our own in the forecastle, and got leave to have it tried. We divided the twenty-four hours into three watches of eight hours each, and the plan, while it allowed us our full share of rest and sleep, gave perfect satisfaction to the master; we returned to port after a very hard season in sound health and in good spirits, without having had one case of sickness among us all the while we were away. And all the voyage we reckoned ourselves rather a jolly crew, and pulled together with a will, when there was extra work to do.

A ship is often in the best possible trim after she has been two or three months at sea. Every chafe has been perfectly served with spun-yarn, or protected by rope mats or 'Scotchmen' (slips of wood or bamboo). The old sails are all mended, the rigging has been completely overhauled, and shrouds and stays set up taut. The yards are painted, the masts scraped and varnished, and the decks have been holystoned until the heads of the copper bolts glisten like overgrown sovereigns that might have been dropped upon the clean white planks. Every inch of standing rigging shines with 'Stockholm;'[7] the bends and anchors are blacked, the sides painted in grinning Quaker port-holes, and the boat-swain's locker is full over the brim with the work of the men's hands in the shape of gaskets, man-ropes, chafing gear, grafted strops, fancy yoke-lines, huge balls of marlin,[8] house-line, spun-yarn, and other blue water manufactures. Then comes the season of what we call humbugging. The master puzzles his head to make work for the crew, rather than case the watches. To annoyances of this kind sailors are more especially subject in ships carrying no passengers. Passengers are a check upon the master; but I have sailed more than once under masters who have needed no check of that kind, and who have been kind and fatherly towards their crews. Then, mind you, nothing to do is as bad for most crews as overwork. Sky-larking and lop-lollying don't improve a man's seamanship; and it is well for him to be kept in regular employ upon some reasonable duty; but that mustn't be overdone. We soon get cantankerous and discontented if we are worried with unnecessary orders, and set to undo to-day what we did yesterday, and persecuted with petty acts of tyranny, which too many skippers are able and glad to exercise.

There is no help, perhaps, against that last trouble; but there should be help against it when either tyranny or want of reasonable care ends in loss of limb or life. If I could catch the ear of any honourable member, I would tell him here is a case in which we forecastle-men think a little interference of the law much wanted. I have seen many a man killed, and I know, and every seaman knows, that a merchantman rarely makes two long voyages together without losing by a casualty at least one of her hands, or having one or more men maimed for life. Many of these accidents are beyond human prevention; but a terrible number of them are produced by culpable deficiencies in spars

---

[7] Stockholm tar: pine tar used in shipbuilding and also in the manufacture and maintenance of cordage.

[8] Marlin, or Marline: cord composed of two strands loosely twisted and either tarred or white, used for winding ropes and cables to prevent their being frayed by blocks etc.

or rigging, or by careless inattention of the officers in foolishly exposing men to danger. The country knows we are no cowards, and we know that there are plenty of fine noble fellows in command of trading vessels; and though I say it, the country should take better care of us.

But there are some in command who are not fine or noble, and there are some good fellows who are careless, and who would be more careful if they were made responsible by the certainty of an inquiry into every case of accidental death on board the ship. If a man is killed ashore, the beadle[9] takes it up, the coroner is informed of it, and goes and sits; the newspapers are told of it, and all the editors are down like boatswains' cats[10] upon anything they see foul in the matter; faulty machinery gets fined, juries storm; and every one ashore takes the very utmost care, if only for his own sake, to keep himself from maiming any fellow-creature. On board ship, how is it? A sailor is killed. Down goes some such entry as this into the log book:—'REMARKS. At six bells in the middle watch, during a heavy squall, John Treenail went out to stow the flying jib. The weather-guy parted; the flapping of the sail sprung the boom, which broke short off, and the man fell overboard. Hove the ship to, but, the boats being stowed on deck, were unable to lower one in time to save him. At seven bells made sail; ship laying her course.' On the arrival of the ship at the next port the lost man's register ticket is given up at the custom-house, and his death reported there. 'The Merchant Seaman's Fund' claims his clothes and wages, if no near relatives appear. Beyond those points no attention is likely to be paid to the matter by the authorities. The man's life in such a case—a sample of a large number of others—was, most likely, lost for want of a few fathom of new rope to replace the worn-out guy [rope]. In men-of-war, where the immediate authorities are more responsible, such accidents don't happen nearly so often, although there the men are required to be much more smart, to show much more agility, and to perform, in fact, more dangerous climbing and skipping up aloft. Many merchant seamen's lives would be saved every year, if there were strict

[9] Beadle: messenger of the Court.

[10] Cat, or Cat-o-nine-tails: a whip consisting of nine knotted pieces of line or cord fastened to a piece of thick rope and used for flogging.

inquiry made at home into the cause of every fatal accident, or serious bodily maiming; and if, in case of proved neglect, a money compensation were made payable by the party in fault to the wounded man, or to the dead man's parents, wife, children, or friends.

As for the more delicate care of the sailor's life, in the way of attending to him when in sickness, I suppose that to be, in a trading vessel without passengers or a surgeon, quite out of the question. A sick sailor at sea is the lame horse of the team. He is in everybody's mess and nobody's watch, and his existence is completely miserable. No lighter diet replaces the customary rough food, and the captain physics him according to a book he carries inside the medicine-chest. Some masters have a taste for surgery and carve their patients most unmercifully; but a blister and a strong dose of salts are the remedies most commonly in use for all complaints, and when they fail, the sick man is happiest who is left to his fate.

I have said nothing about the Twenty-two Fines and other sailors' grievances, because Dorothy has hinted to me that if I go through my list I shall be set down for a regular grumbler, and get nobody to mind what I am saying. So I shall say no more, but just put it to any landsman how *he* would like to board and lodge in a forecastle and keep the watches as we sailors keep them; and whether he would not growl if, on the top of all this aggravation, there were piled coils of laws tier upon tier to keep him down and squeeze the juice out of him for owners to get at it more easily.

Had we been learned and had Brutuses among us, there would long ago have been some oratory and some agitation on these matters; but we are mostly too ignorant to state our case, and there is nobody except ourselves who fairly knows it. I shall write no more; but I wish that somebody who looks out for occasions to do good, would see into these matters for us and tell them in a freshwater way, so as to get attention. Dorothy, by what I read, seems to have put down my statement very well: I thank her for it; but it was not to be expected she could altogether take the brine out of my language. So no more at present.

Only, ladies and gentlemen, when you are thinking—and not without need—about your national defences, I ask you whether these things, though of a common sort, aren't worth considering? You live in an island, you know. You must have sailors. How *can* you keep 'em off so!

Figure 5.4 Shipwreck: Survivors of the emigrant ship *Eric the Red* wrecked off Cape Otway. *Australasian Sketcher*, 11 September 1880.

9

Sailors' Homes Afloat

Samuel Rinder and Henry Morley

Life and conditions on English merchantmen ships.
Volume: 6 Number: 152 Pages: 529–33
Date: February 19, 1853
Fee: 5 pounds for 8 ¼ Columns.

Dorothy my niece, who is a scholar, writes this for me, and puts it into her fine English as I tell it to her in my own salt-water way. I am a fore-mast hand, an able seaman, I can hand,[1] reef,[2] and steer, I can strop[3] a block[4] or turn in a dead-eye;[5] but my fingers are more handy with the tar-pot[6] than the ink-bottle. Many a landsman who would rather ink his hands than tar them,

---

[1] Hand: to furl; to wrap (a sail) close to a yard or mast and fasted it with a gasket. Yard: a slender rod or spar tapered towards the end and fastened at right angles across the mast to support the sail. Gasket: a rope or cord by which a furled sail is tied to the yard.

[2] Reef: cut down the size of a sail by taking in and tying down part of it; also, to lower (a spar; to shorten a mast or bowsprit) by taking part of it in, lowering it etc.

[3] Strop: in rope making, a rope with an eye at both ends, used in twisting strands.

[4] Block: a pulley or system of pulleys mounted on its frame or shell, with its band or strap.

[5] Dead-eye: a round flat wooden block pierced with three holes to receive a lanyard (cord): used on a ship to extend the shrouds and stays for other purposes. Shroud: a set of ropes stretched from the ship's side to the masthead to offset lateral strain on the mast. Stays: strong rope or cable used to support the mast.

[6] Tar: used for preserving and protecting surfaces.

does not know what it is to haul out a weather earing[7] in a gale; I do, so don't let anybody call me ignorant. I'm afraid, too, that I know some other things that are not known on land; for I do think that if what you call the public had properly known before this what I want to tell them now, things wouldn't be exactly what they are as this leaves me at present.

I fancy I catch somebody saying, what don't the public know about them? Sailors, certainly, have had a great deal of attention lately. Perhaps we don't understand it, and so don't like it as we ought to do: I can't say, I am sure. Members of Parliament have gathered all sorts of statistics about us, and we've been obliged to carry bits of paper with our eyes, noses, and mouths, and our blue anchors and ladies on our arms and chests put down in them, and we are forced to keep them, or to lose them at our peril, and otherwise, also, we are legislated for more than enough. We have our own notion of things, and we talk them over in the forecastle.[8] So it comes to pass that I and my shipmates have agreed that we would try and get some of our opinions outspoken somewhere in print, especially about the forecastle itself. For when we see the comfortable Sailor's Homes built up for us ashore, where we spend on an average only about two months in the year, we think there must be many people who don't know how we spend the other ten months of the twelve, and what a need there is of something more comfortable and decent than is now provided for the Sailors' Homes at sea.

I said two months, but I believe it to be mostly not more than six weeks of the twelve-month that a sailor spends ashore, and nearly all the acts of Parliament that go to make us comfortable are intended for the good of us during those six weeks; as for the other forty-six, we are left in those pretty much at the mercy of cargo-loving owners and blue water skippers. A skipper in deep water is commonly less polite and considerate than a skipper in soundings or ashore. It is quite true that the law has ordained how many

---

[7] Earing: a small rope attached to the cringle (a ring of rope or metal) of a sail; or a small rope for attaching a sail to the yard or gaff.

[8] Forecastle (also known as fo'c's'le): the upper deck of a ship in front of the foremast; also, the front part of a merchant ship where the sailors' quarters are located.

ounces of biscuit, beef, peas and lime juice we shall get at sea, and has laid heavy penalties on masters who neglect to furnish the due supply of lime juice. For that much we thank the honourable House of Commons that it has attended a little to the commons of the sailor, but it is our opinion in the forecastle, as I may some day show if I can find a way to talk these matters through and overhaul the Merchant Seaman's Act, that the advantages got out of new laws are ten to the owners and the captain against one to the man before the mast.

Let a man go aboard what merchant ship he will, and after he has seen the cabins for the officers and passengers, ask for a peep at the accommodations that has been provided for the sailors in it. My last voyage was in the *Hope of Plymouth*, a barque that carried emigrants to Melbourne. They are all pretty much alike, I was not worse lodged there than aboard other vessels, but now do just look at what our lodging was. Of course there was the officer's home under the poop,[9] with a painted and carved front, and brass rods like the outside of a caravan, all snug inside, well lighted, with table, chairs, sofas, ingenious lockers and books. The mizzen mast[10] that rose through the farther end was disguised with fine carving and painting. Doors led from the cabin to the officers' berths in little state-rooms well lighted, carpeted, and comfortable. We don't grudge our officers any comfort, and we don't want any carving, painting, or carpeting for ourselves. Let gentlemen be gentlemen, and men be men, but don't kennel the men like dogs. Well, then, if we left the cabin and went down the after-hatchway to the 'tween decks; there we found the emigrants. They are badly enough lodged in some vessels, but aboard the *Hope* their passage money had been paid by Government, and they were well looked after. They occupied the whole length of the ship, that was divided for them into three separate homes; that to the fore for single men, the after one for single women and the hospital, with the seagoing

---

[9] Poop: a raised deck at the stern of a ship, and sometimes forming the roof of a cabin: also poop deck.

[10] Mizzen: the mast nearest the stern on a ship with two masts. It holds the fore and aft mizzen sails.

home for married folk between the two. They had tables, benches, shelves, lamps, and such things. They had sleeping berths in two tiers with room for a man to settle comfortably down or sit upright in any one of them. They got light through strong panes of glass in the ship's sides, and bull's eyes in the deck overhead. Their place was ventilated at some cost, and as the Emigration Commissioners insisted on seven feet of clear space between the decks, they could let their tables down by the hinges, and have exercise during wet weather. Acts of Parliament regulate the amount of space each emigrant shall have, the quality as well as quantity of food to be provided, even when he shall get up and go to bed. That is all very good and very wise.

I mind me that I sailed in 1837 from Liverpool to New York with Irish emigrants when there was no such care taken, and the people, having merely paid the passage money, found their own provisions. The poor creatures took chiefly potatoes, eggs, and oatmeal, and few took more than enough to last them through an average passage. The ship got into heavy weather and the voyage lasted eight weeks: no extraordinary time, but long enough to cause a famine. We got into New York with more than two-thirds of our emigrants depending for life upon a biscuit and two or three dried sprats daily. The ship's stores could not furnish more, and as it was it was found necessary to arm the crew and garrison the cabin, that we might prevent the poor hungry souls from breaking the store rooms open. I remember, too, what we all suffered on a voyage to Port Phillip with emigrants, in 1840. The vessel touched at the Cape for water, and the skinflint of an agent who was a passenger in her, prevented the captain from laying in a full supply. The consequence was that long before we made the coast of New Holland, each man's daily allowance was reduced from six pints to two, and then to one pint. At length we were obliged to alter our course and bear up for King George's Sound, near Swan River, for water. Off the entrance of the harbour the ship lay for three days becalmed under a roasting sun. The men went out in boats prospecting in vain for springs upon the sandy shore. There was not a drop of water on board ship during those three days. Two children died of thirst. Men lay moaning about the decks. The cause of our distress shut himself up in the cabin, where he had no lack of bottled ale and soda water. A breeze that sprang up on the fourth day carried us through the long sound, and as we got into the narrow channel leading to the inner harbour, a boat from Albany—where the report of our signal guns had at length been heard—boarded us, and the crew, finding our condition, pulled off to the nearest spring, laden with kegs and buckets.

The strict regulations now enforced prevent such scenes from occurring any more in emigrant ships, but in vessels carrying merely their crews—merely as sailors, for whose home afloat nobody has yet begun to care—they are common enough. In the very last vessel of the kind to which I belonged, the *Abbots Reading* of Liverpool, after a very quick passage from South America, we came in sight of the Azores, with no other provisions on board than biscuits, beans, and water. Very good provender for horses, but not quite the right fare for hard-working men.

Well, then, to go back to the *Hope*, there is all that care taken on board an emigrant vessel—and very properly taken too—of men whose whole experience of sea-going does not come to more than a few months in all their knowledge. What sort of care is taken of the men who live aboard ship, sometimes by the year together, and during all the chief part of their lives?

In old-fashioned ships the forecastle is beneath the main-deck, but as it there occupies space which may be profitably given up to cargo, it is now, in almost all large vessels, superseded by the top-gallant[11] forecastle. The top-gallant forecastle of the *Hope*, which is a fair sample of the Sailors' Home at sea, was made, as usual, in manner following. In the fore part of the ship a second deck was laid, about five feet above the main deck, reaching as far aft as the windlass, and thus covering that part of the ship included in the round sweep of the bows. Under this roofing a low cavern was formed, about eighteen feet wide at the entrance, and gradually narrowing to a point at the other end. The extreme length of it was eighteen or twenty feet, and it was barely five feet high between the beams. A landsman might compare this kind of sailors' home to the inside of a large baker's oven. In this top-gallant forecastle, containing less space and less air than is the Government

---

[11] Top-gallant: any part of a ship (mast, sail, spar, forecastle etc.) situated higher, or elevated above the adjoining part of the ship.

allowance for two solitary cells in Pentonville Prison, sixteen people were to eat, drink, and sleep, and keep their clothes, and make themselves at home with one another. It was the whole lodging provided for the carpenter, nine seamen, five boys, and the cook, that being the complement of hands on board the *Hope*, or any other vessels of four hundred and sixty tons register.

The front of this home of ours was boarded off across its whole breadth, and was to be entered on each side by a sliding door. The anchor chains having passed through doors of their own—two large square holes, left in the front for that purpose—ran along the whole length of the forecastle, to be carried through the hawse-holes[12] and shackled to the anchors. As this ground tackle must be always ready for instant use when the ship is near land, these four holes were at such times left open: one pair of them let in the wind, the other pair the water. We had no windows, and could get light only when the doors were open. In rough weather, however, if we did not keep the doors carefully shut, a large part of every sea that washed the decks would give our forecastle a rinsing. The two doorways, when fully open, were each of them about four feet high, and just wide enough to allow a man to squeeze in and out sideways.

Of course, by habit, we could all learn to squeeze into our dark hole without knocking our heads over much against the upper deck. A wife from shore if she came in to see one of us, supposing she was clever enough at stooping,—for in our homes at sea no full-grown person can stand upright—would soon bruise her shins in the dark, over our chests strewn about the floor. If she was a tidy woman, she would pine a bit to see the sort of home her Bill had got into. Down the middle of the hole that is allotted, let me say again, to sixteen people, she would see, as soon as her eyes could cut a way into the gloom, a great spar four or five feet round, the heel of the bowsprit,[13] with a pair of bunks fixed on each side

---

[12]Hawse: the neck part of the forecastle or bow of a ship.
Hawse-hole: one of the holes in the bow of a ship through which a cable passes: also, the space between the bow of a ship and the anchors.

[13] Bowsprit: a large tapered pole or plank extended forward from the bow of a sailing vessel. The foremost stays are fastened to it.

Figure 5.5 Furling sail, c.1800s. *Jack Tar: A Sailor's Life 1750–1910*, Woodbridge: Antique Collectors' Club, 1999.

of it, dividing the place into two equal parts. Here are bunks, of course, or berths as you call them, fixed against the walls, and anybody standing in one of the halves of the forecastle might rest an elbow on each wall of berths. But there is not clear deck even in that little compass, for there are two rows of chests further blocking up the space, and the clear deck on either side of the bowsprit is a lane only about twelve inches wide. So merchant sailors lodge,—so we were accommodated in the *Hope*; two of us could not pass unless one mounted a chest and crouched upon it. When the cables were bent, we had not even our twelve inches of floor: the muddy chains then rested on the only vacant planks, and there was no rest for the sole of the sailor's foot upon the floor of his own home.

The bunks in which we slept were no worse than I have found sailor's beds to be on board most vessels in the merchant service. There were two tiers of them on each side, three in each tier; those twelve, with the four fixed on the heel of the bowsprit, made up our number. Each bunk was barely six feet long, and twenty inches wide. The height of the whole forecastle being only about five feet, we had less than two feet space between one bunk, and the vent above it. I slept in an upper bunk, using the heel of a studding-sail[14] boom for a pillow. My nose, when I had got between the blankets, was within three inches of the beam that crossed above me, and if ever I forgot myself and tried to raise my head at all, without first pushing it out beyond the side board, I was punished for my want of thought. Then when I went to bed, of course a little skill was necessary to get into it at all. I had to put my elbow into one end of the bunk, and my heel over the other end, raise my body into a horizontal position, and then slide myself in sideways, by a wriggling motion that it's not in my power verbally to explain. Once in, stretched on his back, with his broad shoulders firmly wedged between the ship's timbers on one side and the outer board on the other; his head threatened with bruise or breakage if he raises it incautiously;—the seaman a-bed in his sea-going home must lie as though he were fixed snugly in his coffin. The luxury of drawing his knees up to his chin, and coiling himself snugly in the blankets, is of course quite out of the question.

So we were lodged aboard the *Hope*. The-hawse holes through which the chain passes, being only plugged up in a temporary way with old tarpaulin, let in water every time the ship dipped her nose into the sea. The water

[14] Studding-sail: a light sail set at the side of the principal square sail of a vessel in free winds to increase the speed. Studding-sail boom: a long spar (pole) set to project from a ship to extend the foot of a sail.

reached the main deck through a small scupper[15] hole beneath the bunks, and as the vessel pitched, came back into the forecastle none the cleaner for its travels. In this way there was kept up a continual wash on the lee-side[16] of the room, not well relished by those of the crew whose beds and blankets now and then were wetted by it. Then again, through each of the two lower foremost bunks there passed a mass of timber and copper bolts, forming part of the cat-heads.[17] The seams surrounding the cat-heads being at most times leaky from the working of the ship, a cool salt stream was generally trickling through them, so that the tenants of those two bunks had both jam and pickle.[18] From the crevices around the iron spindle of the capstan and the timber bits, two other rivulets flowed slowly down the bowsprit and across the narrow floor, spreading beneath the chests, rotting their bottoms, and quietly destroying our chief articles of property, namely, our shore-going suits of clothes.

I have sailed in some vessels, and I know that there are many, in which the forecastle does not contain so many bunks as bodies. Some of the crew agree then to 'turn in and out,' two men in different watches keeping the same berth warm. In harbour, when all hands are below together, some of the crew are, in such a case, compelled to sleep on chests.

Never did anybody, poet or romancing man, describe a den that could be worse than a top-gallant forecastle during a gale of wind or a long spell of dirty weather. The men get wet through in every watch, and hang up their wet clothes, as they come in, on nails driven into the beams. They steam like soup and flavour our darkness with a moist and nasty taste. The doors are kept well closed to bar out the heavy sprays that dash against them, and the

---

[15] Scupper: a drainage hole cut through the side of a ship flush with the deck.

[16] Lee-side: relating to the sheltered side from the wind, as opposed to the weather-side.

[17] Cat-head: a projecting piece of timber or iron near the bow of a ship to which the anchor is hoisted and secured.

[18] 'Jam and pickle': jam—wedge in a tight space; Pickle—salt water solution for preserving meat and fish; also relating to being in trouble or a predicament (triple pun probably intended).

forecastle is pitch dark day and night, except when a man slips in with the water at his heels, and shuts the slide up suddenly.

Well, that's the forecastle. That is the sailor's home at sea. When your landsmen sing, as I hear butcher boys do, how they're afloat, they're afloat on the fierce rolling tide, the ocean's their home, and the bark is their bride, I hope they'll take these words of an old sailor to heart, and think what sort of a home they would get upon the ocean in a merchant's barque,[19] more especially if there was a particularly rolling sea. That's the sort of place we merchant sailors live in when we are at home; as for your sailors' homes ashore, they're very good; but we don't live in them long enough; we can't carry them aboard. If the honourable House that has looked a little to our commons, would just legislate a little humanely for the lodging of the common seaman on board ship, just as it has legislated for the lodging of the emigrants—if an Inspector were required to step down into every forecastle before a trader left port—I don't think there would be a very wrong thing done. But then I'm a forecastle man myself, and dare say I'm ignorant and don't properly consider owners' interests, and then don't rightly feel that the size of the cargo is of more worth than the health and comfort of the crew.

Now I have something to say about the common seaman's victuals. Parliament regulates the quantity, but quality depends upon the pocket of the ship-owner. In some London ships I know, and I dare say in a few ships from other ports, the provisions supplied are excellent; but in most English vessels, and especially in those from other ports than London, they are either second-rate or bad. My teeth are most used to such biscuit as would never be put on board an American trader, nor on board many Scotch ships. Salt-beef is known justly in the merchant service as salt-horse or mahogany.[20] Every cask of mahogany is opened in the presence of the steward, who picks out the good bits for the cabin, and leaves the worst for us forecastle men. Our tea—our greatest luxury—is of the cheapest and coarsest kind. Masters, mates, men-of-war's men, emigrants, and convicts, are all supplied with preserved

---

[19] Barque (bark): a three masted vessel with its foremast and mainsail square rigged and mizzen-mast fore and aft rigged.

[20] Mahogany: reddish-brown hardwood.

meats, soups, vegetables, &c.; but anything of that kind is as rare a sight upon the English merchant seaman's chest, as turtle soup upon a tradesman's dinner-table. In spite of all improvements, and all new preparations, there has been little change made in the kind of provisions supplied to us during the last half century, except that we have had our grog stopped, and got nothing in its place.

Of course we may get hardened by usage to this kind of treatment, but we are not too stupid to make comparisons, and as some of us have seen a little of the Yankee vessels—I for one—we grumble; we grumble, even, dissatisfied wretches, at the savage way in which we are obliged to eat our food. We want to sit before it like Christians, but can't. Tables are impossible in our small den, and we know no more than the wolves do about table knives and forks. The pork and pea-soup, or beef and rice are served up in small tubs, which pass round from hand to hand. Each pours his allowance of soup or rice into a tin pot, and eats his bit of meat out of the lump with the clasp-knife that hangs about his neck. Breakfast and supper are alike with us; we get a quart of black mess mixed with small twigs and 'cabbage,' and in that we soak our brown and flinty (if not always chalky) biscuit, fishing up the pieces with the points of our knives.

Just now I said that I had seen a little of the way the Yankees treat their sailors. I will tell in a few words what the sailor's home is aboard the best American ships. Some few English owners, I am told, have followed the example. From the break of the poop to the hawse-holes the deck is flush, unbroken, on both sides. The forecastle is on the same level as the waist, and guarded by high bulwarks[21] that shelter the men well. In the middle of the deck there is a round wooden building called the Round-house, where the crew are lodged. The roof is dome-shaped, and so gives height to the room within, which is six feet high round the sides, and eight feet in the middle. The tallest of the seamen walks erect in it. This place is fitted up with berths, much like those in our forecastles, only more roomy and comfortable. Every berth is lighted by a little window, beneath which there is a long shelf, or rather a narrow cupboard, divided into several compartments and closed by

---

[21] Bulwarks: the side of a ship above the upper deck.

a door with hinges to it. Along the front of each berth hangs a curtain, making it completely private.

In the middle of the round-house is a table with ledges round it, to prevent dishes from slipping off, and about the table there is fixed a broad bench, upon which the seamen sit down properly to dinner. There is another bench, too, running along the edge of the lower bunks. Beneath the bench that goes about the table there are lockers that contain a good supply of knives and forks and spoons, and things that civilised men who live ashore use at their dinner. Their solid food is brought to the men on board these Yankee vessels in bright metal dishes, and their soup—in a tureen! The men, instead of tearing the tough beef to pieces with their fingers, as we do in English forecastles—where we must sit as we can, with little piles of broken biscuit on the ground beside us—the men in the round-house[22] sit down ship-shape at table, handling their knives and forks over a piece of 'prime mess' that has come after a course of fresh 'soup and bouilli,'[23] and that is made sweet and wholesome by the help of a dish of dried potatoes, and by a good supply of pepper, mustard, and pickles. Those are articles of which every sea-going man knows the value, but which are rarely given to us English seamen. The house itself of the American sailors has a clean, wholesome, homely look. It is large enough to lodge properly the whole ship's company; and it is well lighted and warmed. A lamp hangs from a small skylight, protected by strong wire and a good stove is part of the home furniture.

It is very well to tell us, as some English owners do, that these round-houses interfere with the working of the ship, are liable to be washed overboard, and so on. We know what that means. And we ask any landsmen who will take my word, as he may safely, for the condition of an English top-gallant forecastle, if it is wonderful that we desert our vessels, and prefer good pay, and good lodging, in the American merchant service? A power of laws are made to stop desertion, and to keep us to the English ships by

---

[22] Round-house: a cabin or apartment in the after part of the quarter-deck having the poop for its roof.

[23] Bouilli: boiled beef.

penalties and threats. But give us a law or two designed to make the English ships better worth stopping in, and you will give us something worth having—and give England something worth having too.

10
The Life of Poor Jack [Conditions of Seamen][1]
Henry Morley

Conditions suffered by seamen on board merchant ships with a plea for government to enact regulations to protect seamen, and in particular, for those laws to be enforced. Some reference to Australia.
Volume: 7 Number: 165 Pages: 286–88
Date: May 21, 1853
Fee: No fee for 6 Columns.

With respect to the remarks made by a tar[2] in your honoured journal, I am appointed secretary to a committee of old salts, respectable friends who smoke their pipes together at times in my crib,[3] of which I give you the address in confidence, where we shall be glad to see you any Tuesday after six in this month, which are open evenings, and no charge for your beer. Having a little property by right of my wife which was an upper servant in the Savings Bank, I left the sea myself a many years ago, not liking to eat mahogany[4] and do the work of an elephant upon the keep and lodging of a pig. My position in society as landlord of *The Tar Ashore,* requires that I should be current in the salt-water talk of landsmen, and overhaul the log of parliament both as regards debates and blue books,[5]

---

[1] Jack (also, Jack-tar): a sailor.
[2] Tar: (see above) a sailor.
[3] Crib: public house.
[4] Mahogany: euphemism for dried meat (alluding to the red-brown hardwood of the same name).
[5] Blue books: government publication providing information; usually detailed government reports.

which my wife, to whom I read the interesting parts aloud, says are blue bores, and she hopes will some day choke me. That, however, properdebots as the French say.[6]

When the remarks made by a tar in your honoured journal being read from the chair in our committee, were approved as correct, it was considered that there were some more facts that might be submitted to your readers. Consequently I was authorised to draw up this communication, of which you are at liberty to make what use you please.

Concerning what was said about crews being compelled to sail in unseaworthy vessels, I am directed to send you without comment this paragraph, which Tom Winkle cut yesterday out of the Bristol Mercury, for April 23, 1853:—

THE JANE.—From a report in the Commercial Rooms we perceive that the Jane, which left this port on Wednesday se'nnight[7] for Quebec, has put back to King Road. It will be remembered that on Tuesday, the 12th instant, the crew, consisting of fourteen men, were brought before the magistrates for refusing to go to sea in this vessel. The men gave as a reason that she was not sea-worthy, but the magistrate did not consider the case made out on the part of the men, and *committed them to prison for fourteen days.* The Jane IS LEAKY, and we learn that she will have to discharge her cargo, and go into Messrs. Hill's dock for repair.—*Bristol Mercury*, April 23, 1853.

Something was said of undermanning vessels, and the entering of fishmongers, tailors, and others, who desired to work their passage out to the gold diggings, at a reduced pay, to the hurt of good seamen by lowering their rate of wages, and screwing up to the worst possible pinch their rate of work. It might have been said—for it is true—that vessels, undermanned already, carry out among their crews men taking a passage in the forecastle (where their mothers may pity them, but sailors don't) entered and bound to work, who receive not a farthing for their labour. Matthew Crab, one of our set,

---

[6] Properdebots: probably a corruption of Latin/French; possibly relating to bots, or intestinal worms which can eventually choke a person.

[7] Se'nnight (also, se'n-night): seven nights; the space of seven days and seven nights.

who has just come home from Australia, says, and is ready to testify, that there were two men in the forecastle of his vessel who came on board with hands like satin. One of them was a gentleman; the other was a Scotch tobacconist; they had both been cleaned out at the diggings and could see no other way of getting home. If the forecastle was not quite so terrible a den, and a three months' voyage, with common sailor's board and lodging, was not so very much worse than three months in the filthiest old jail in England, there would be no need of professed sailors at all. There are lots of men wanting to go somewhere who wouldn't mind taking the command of a ship, to say nothing of working in her. The two men who sailed with Crab were to get no wages at all, though they were took on board and put into the berths of seamen. Hard berths they were. The gentleman, says Crab, showed he was well bred, for he made himself agreeable, ran up the rigging, and pulled at the ropes his best. He was worth some of the salt he didn't get, and the men treated him civilly. The tobacconist did nothing but growl about his kennel like an ugly dog, and a dog's life he had to lead for it. He always was the horse that never pulled; he only shammed work, and every bit of strength he should have used had to be put out extra by the other men, who would have been short-handed enough, even if both the land lubbers had been A. B.'s.[8] As it is obvious to the meanest understanding you, I am sure, will see that by acting in this way owners or masters place themselves upon the horns of a dilemma. If it be said that men who work their passage in that way are fit for the work, I ask, why are they not paid? If it be said that they are not fit for the work, I ask, sir, why are they taken? As the Ghost says in the comedy, I pause for a reply. If any, speak!

I fear it is of no use speaking, but I will reply myself. Vessels are manned anyhow, because there is money made by cutting down the cost of hands, and the risk run by so doing is not run by the owner. And insurance covers it. Vessels that go out well insured, may often make a quicker and a better voyage to the bottom than to any distant port. Though nobody would be so wicked as to turn them adrift wilfully, with a design that they should run

[8] A.B's: able-bodied seaman.

Figure 5.6 Galley on board the *Union of London*, 1823. *Jack Tar: A Sailor's Life 1750–1910,* Woodbridge: Antique Collectors' Club, 1999.

astray or founder, very few owners let their sleep be broken much with dreading of the chance of a wrecked vessel. If babies in short clothes wanted to go out as mariners with short wages, and their mothers would let 'em, there would be no want of owners careless enough to entrust vessels to their keeping. The consequence of all this carelessness is, as I find in my blue books, that of every seventeen sailors who die, twelve are drowned or lost by shipwreck. Two thousand of us go to the bottom yearly; and I should like somebody to count how many women have the thought of a dead sailor curled up in their hearts, and how many sailors' orphans there are in the workhouses and gutters.

I am advised to speak by book, for the Committee says to me, 'We are ignorant men, and the public may suppose it to be ignorance that makes us grumble. Give them out some of your learning, Cockle.' Now, I've been thumbing an official report, in which I find the evidence of a gentleman who spoke exactly what we know—an honourable captain who had served both in the navy and the merchant seaman's service—he was a man to be well informed, and so he was. Well, what did he say? 'No one,' he said, 'can go into the City, or have transactions with the fitting out of merchant ships, without witnessing, in daily transactions, the fatal extent of the carelessness which prevails in the selection of the master, officers and men, and in the equipment of merchant vessels. Any man who can procure a loading for the vessel from any foreign port will seldom be refused the appointment of master, or have any inquiry made into his character. I have even known a Portsmouth publican who commanded a vessel trading from Lisbon to London.' Now, what do you think of that? Not but what a publican's business is exceedingly respectable; but, because he had sold wine in a sea-port town, was that brother victualler to be considered qualified to take a ship to Lisbon? He had not, it is farther said, the most distant conception of his duty as a captain, but he trusted in such knowledge as had been picked up at sight by one of the common seamen who sailed with him. The same witness and honourable captain, who had often crossed the seas as a passenger, able to observe with a professional eye the doings of the sailors, gave an edifying list of his experiences, such as might be given by any man equally qualified to criticise, who travels much on the high seas. He sailed once from London with ninety persons in a steam-vessel (of course, highly insured) commanded by an ignorant sot, whose character could never have endured an hour's inquiry.

At the request of officers and crew the naval passenger took the command out of his hands; and the commander appointed by the owners, when he got ashore, cut his throat in a fit of drunken delirium. The honourable captain came home from Cape Finisterre[9] to London once in a brig of two hundred tons, and found the second mate the only man on board who knew a morsel about navigation. The vessel made Cape Clear[10] instead of the Land's End.[11] The honourable captain once came to England in a brig so disgracefully undermanned, that it could afford only two hands to each watch. In a squall at night the helmsman often was obliged to leave the ship unsteered, while he went forward to let go ropes. In a moderate gale off Cape St. Vincent[12] a fore-topsail had to be cut away from the yard, because, with three men and two boys in a vessel of two hundred and fifty tons, it was not possible to furl it. These are bits of the experience of a single gentleman. If an able mariner took notes in that way of the manning and seamanship on board every merchant vessel, and the tales of all the vessels were to be told once a twelvemonth, we should only wonder that the yearly loss of property by shipwreck should be so little as three million; that the loss of British trading vessels should not be much greater than one in twenty-four; that, out of every seventeen sailors, there should be as many as five who are not lost on the broad sea, but die like other people. Twenty thousand sailors, every ten years, is a mere trifle of men to have cut off in the prime of life—tumbled from mast-heads, cast among savages, or drowned among the smash of ships, illmastered and ill-manned.

I think, therefore, and our committee thinks, that the wish expressed by the tar in your honoured journal, for the establishment of a system of compensation for every preventable mishap on board ship, for every life lost in a ship proved to be badly navigated, or defective in its make or manning, would compel owners to look alive, as nothing else will. Sympathy is too cheap; people don't mind having to sympathise, where they would not at all like having to pay. I would make every man responsible in his pocket for the loss he inflicts on others by neglecting proper precautions against damage to

[9] Cape Finisterre: north-western coast of Spain.

[10] Cape Clear Island: off the south-west coast of Ireland.

[11] Lands End: south-western tip of England.

[12] Cape St Vincent: south-western tip of Portugal.

his fellow-creatures in the carrying on of his business, or in doing of anything whatever that he may do. Whether they be railway directors, builders, manufacturers, farmers, or ship-owners, let them be compelled to make good to widows or children of men killed or damaged in their service, the money value of the support thus taken from them. I see by my books that there is a rule of this kind in the French Civil Code, which has three articles, as follows:

'Art. 1382. Every act whatsoever of the man who occasions a damage to another, obliges him by whose fault it happens to repair it.

'Art. 1383. Every one is responsible for the damage he has caused, not only by his act, but by his negligence or by his imprudence.

'Art. 1384. A man is responsible not only for the damage occasioned by his own act, but also for that which is occasioned by the act of persons for whom he should answer, or of things which he has in his charge.'

The above responsibility holds good unless the persons answerable for each case of damage, prove that they were unable to hinder the act that gave rise to it. Now, almost every act of bad seamanship could be hindered by ship-owners, if they subjected their officers to strict examination, and took proper care to entrust their vessels to fit men, and to a sufficient number of them. The money responsibility, in the case of ships, might be arranged equitably to fall, according to the nature of the accident, on officer or owner, but men should be made careful of the lives of their neighbours or dependants upon peril of their pockets, or they never will be half particular enough. When inquiry was made into the causes of accident in mines, a little fact was elicited that proves this cleverly. In certain mines of a moderate depth, though a life was lost, or a limb shattered whenever a rope broke, the ropes were found to be pieced with iron clamps, and patched and pieced again, to save the cost of new ones. In deeper mines, where the breakage of the long rope caused a more serious loss and stoppage of important works, patched ropes were seldom found; they were renewed regularly at short intervals. Or, take another illustration. In making a railway bank, the man who tips earth over the embankment runs with the waggon and gets before the horse to detach it near the edge. The rapid twisting movements necessary, and the unsafe footing, often cause the man who has this duty to do to fall across the rail, and to be crushed or maimed under the truck laden with some three or four tons of earth. Thirteen years ago an assistant-engineer on the Great Western Railway, Mr. Butler Williams, invented a very simple contrivance, which at the cost of ten shillings saves the labour of this man altogether, and enables the driver to detach the horse himself. Very few railways have concerned themselves to think about adopting the contrivance, for the occasional deaths under the old system are casualties of which the weight falls only upon the orphans and widows of the killed. If they were them-selves charged with the cash value of every life or limb lost on the works, as they would be in France, they would be glad enough to keep their eye upon all methods of reducing such an item of expenditure. Death comes to be noticed seriously by a man of business when the old skeleton mounts one of his office stools, now and then, to put down debtor entries in the ledger. He becomes a nuisance who must be himself put down as thoroughly as possible.

If loss of life at sea were money loss to the person hiring and exposing it to risk, there would be some care taken in the selection not only of officers, but of men. Owners would be careful always to send out crews not likely to bring their vessels into danger. Now, the worst men get the most employment, because they are cheap. Educated seamen are not wanted and they are not made. As long ago as the year 1819 there was an effort made to get up an institution for the instruction of sea-boys and apprentices who had been taught by the experience of one voyage the use of knowledge. Nobody encouraged it. Owners as a class don't care for education, because, as matters now stand, they gain nothing by it. If they had to pay compensation to the widows and orphans of the sailors drowned every year through incompetence and carelessness, they would not run the risk of shipping even a single blockhead. An ignorant man placed to look out for land, requires the keeping of a sharp look out upon himself, or he will go to sleep and put the ship in peril through the mere weight of his stupidity. The educated man will generally do his duty, and require but little overlooking. It is the ignorant man who will save trouble to himself, and will be glad when he can cheat the mate, and so escape a little duty. In setting up a shroud or a stay, he will make all so that it looks secure, but, if not closely watched, he will most likely—to get his work over—shirk the proper fastening of the end of the lanyard. The safety of the mast and therefore of the vessel is imperilled; he may know that, but he knows it dimly; at any rate, he is too stupid to reflect upon it or to act upon his knowledge.

Says the captain before quoted, 'When a general casualty happens at sea, if the ship is in danger, the first danger the captain has to arrest is from the ignorance of the men. His first anxiety will perhaps be to have the spirit casks stove in, to prevent the men getting at them; and, if defeated in the attempt, the ignorant men will be the first to rush to get into the boats and cut them away, by which their own danger is increased. You are never free, in cases of emergency, from the dangers of the panics of ignorance.'

Having received myself a liberal education, which enables me to keep up the status I do among the frequenters of The Tar Ashore, I do feel very much shocked at the ignorance of sailor boys and sailor men. Enlarge among their employers the sense of responsibility for life and limb, by putting them to a small corresponding risk of pounds and shillings, and the sweet little cherub will come down from aloft that keeps watch for the life of poor Jack, and set about a little active business with a view to taking care that Jack's alive as long as possible. Some little care will then be taken to train and protect seamen, who shall by all means continue to wear hearts of oak, but cease to carry wooden heads to match them. These are the opinions which I am requested to transmit to you and sign, on behalf of our committee, AHOLIJAH COCKLE.[13]

Mrs. Cockle begs her kind regards.

---

[13] Aholijah could be interpreted to be: 'A-holi-jah'—(Jah, mean Jehovah), or—'a holy Jehovah'—as a euphemism for preacher or sermonizer. A cockle or cockle-boat is a small shallow boat.

Notes

Aholijah Cockle: Dickens loved quirky or witty titles and puns. He worked hard on his characters names enjoying names that expressed some sort of commentary about the character, or conveyed some extra meaning.

The name Aholijah has the hallmarks of one of Dickens' made-up names. He would have expected the same attention given to names by staff writers such as Morley.

11
Chip: Voices from the Deep
Henry Morley

Sailors' grievances: letters from readers in response to previously published articles.[1]
Volume: 8 Number: 197 Page: 424
Date: December 31, 1853
Fee: No fee for 1 ½ Columns.

There have drifted ashore to us a chip or two sent over ships' sides. One is a letter from a master mariner at the Antipodes, evoked by two former articles in this journal.[2] The master mariner not only confirms the account that has been given in these pages of the 'Sailors' Homes Afloat', but even reveals to us, below the lowest deep depicted there, a lower deep. Worse than the top-gallant, he says, is the lower fore-castle.

The main thing to be seen to by any man who desires to advocate the cause of the seaman is, says our friend, 'better house-room, that when they are off duty, they may have a place somewhat fit for a human being to live in. Act of Parliament says they are to have nine feet of deck space; now, any one that knows anything of shipboard, must be aware that this is not enough when it is measured, as it is in a ship's forecastle, with the round of the bow and chain-cables going through it. Any respectable sailor-man always has a chest to hold his clothes, &c., and I have frequently been obliged to allow some of them to put their chests below, away from the place they live in, to

[1] 'Sailors' Homes Afloat', *Household Words*, Vol. 6, p. 529; see also p. 68 in this volume and 'The Life of Poor Jack', *Household Words*, Vol. 7, p. 286; see also p. 81 in this volume.

[2] [Original footnote] See page 529, vol. 6 and page 286, vol. 7.

make room for the others. Only give the British seaman better accommodation on board his vessel, be a little more liberal in his dietary scale, and there would not, I venture to say, be one complaint for every hundred there are at the present time.'

We think there would not.

Another chip comes from an Englishman who has picked up experience on board vessels belonging to the United States navy, and speaks of such a visit as it is in the power of every courteous Englishman visiting America to pay to any fire-spitter that sails under the stars and stripes. 'I found the officers much more civil and good-natured than our own. Captain Fitz-premier would think that a mere traveller in search of information ought to go to blue books, and he would resent the intrusion of a strange man with a card upon the quarter-deck. Captain Cheke, however, of New York, was ready to give information to the full extent of his own knowledge.

'A regulation in America forbids the navy to employ seamen not subjects of the United States. Immense numbers of Her Majesty's lieges, and of those she may one day be ill able to spare, continue to evade this regulation, and obtain employment as Americans. The United States Government pays able-bodied seamen about two pounds a month, and allows to them such superabundant rations that ten men usually live upon the food of eight: they mess together and receive the difference in money. Their pay is, however, generally kept in arrear to prevent desertion; advances are never made. The Americans are in one point quite as weak as we; they fire a great many useless salutes, and every time a gun is discharged four-fifths of a dollar fly away in smoke out of the American treasury.'

We are to be tempted into no remarks of our own upon the British Admiralty, and the perfection at which by long practice its workmen have arrived in the art of sawing ships asunder. We have produced our chips wet from the sea, and will not let them become dry over the heat of what might prove a tedious discussion.

12
Black-Skin Ahead! [Whaling]
Samuel Rinder

Description of a whaling expedition thirty days south of Hobart.
Volume: 6 Number: 146 Pages: 399–404
Date: January 8, 1853
Fee: 3 pounds 3 shillings for 8 Columns.

If there be any man, woman, or child alive who is not satiated with accounts of the South Sea whale fishery, will he, she, or it, be good enough to read what follows.

Thirty days out from Hobart Town, our vessel floated under an unbroken arch of pure blue sky, clear and translucent. On the distant horizon rested the light trade-wind clouds reflecting all the splendour of the rising sun. The quiet dreamy beauty of the scene was indescribable—so I am saved the trouble of describing it. The helmsman felt it and leaned sleepily against the wheel. The officer of the watch shut his eyes to it and nodded on the sky-light. I, with head and arms resting on the bulwarks,[1] was chewing a quid,[2] when from the topmast crosstrees[3] a clear voice rang out, 'There she spouts! Black-skin a-head! There, there she blows again!'—'Where away?' shouted the mate.—'Three points on the weather bow. Hurrah! There she breaches clean out! Single spouts—a school of sparms!' The quiet people of the ship were wakened up as though they had all suddenly been galvanized, and

---

[1] Bulwarks: sides of the ship above the upper deck.

[2] Quid: a piece of tobacco chewed or rolled about the mouth.

[3] Crosstrees: two short horizontal bars across a ship's masthead which spreads the rigging that supports the mast.

jumped about with a delirious activity. The captain rushed up half-dressed from his cabin, with one side of his face elaborately lathered, and a little rivulet of blood trickling from the other. The men blocked up the fore scuttle,[4] and tumbled over each other in their eagerness to reach the deck. Then followed rapid orders, rapidly executed. The ship, which had been slipping along under double-reefed[5] topsail, foresail, and mizzen,[6] was easily hove to. 'Haul up the foresail! Back the mainyard! Pass the tubs into the boats. Bear a hand, and jump in! See the tackle falls clear. Ready?'—'Ay, ay, sir; all ready!'—'Lower away!' The falls whizzed through the davit heads; the men, already seated at their oars, struck out the instant the boats touched the water. Among the men who struck out I was one, and I was then about for the first time to commit assault and battery against the monarch of the sea, and help, if possible, to part leviathan among the merchants.

I take upon myself now to describe a whale boat. South Sea whalers may be distinguished at sea by their boats; they usually carry five, sometimes seven, hung over the side by tackles attached to wooden or iron cranes, called davits,[7] the bow of each boat hanging from one davit and the stern from another. The tackle falls are carefully coiled upon the davits,82 so that they can be let go with a certainty of running clear; and to the bottom of the tackle blocks is attached a weight which instantly unhooks them when the boat touches the water. The boats are of peculiar shape; made low, and of great beam amidships, they gradually taper towards each end. Head and stern are alike, both sharp as a wedge, and raised by a gentle curve which traverses the whole length of the boat. The whale boats, being made in this way, are nearly flat-bottomed in the middle, and have little hold of the water.

---

[4] Scuttle: a small opening or hatchway in the deck of a ship large enough to admit a man; also, a hole in the side or bottom of a ship; or a hole through the coverings of its hatchway.

[5] To reef: to cut down the size of a sail by taking in and tying down part of it.

[6] Mizen (or mizzen) mast: the mast supporting the mizzen sails; the mast that stands nearest the stern of a ship with two or three sails.

[7] Davit: a fixed or movable crane that projects over the side of a ship or over a hatchway and is used for hoisting ship's boats, anchors, or cargo.

Their light build, sharp stems, and rounded sides, give them great swiftness; and their width and low centre of gravity cause them to be, when properly managed, very safe. They are steered by a long and heavy oar, which passes through a rope strap attached to the stern-post. The long leverage gives to the steersman great power over his boat, and enables him to alter her direction, or to turn her round in far less time than if he used the common rudder. In the stern of the boat is fixed a strong, round piece of timber called the loggerhead, to which the towing rope is affixed, and which also serves to check the line when fast to a whale. The head-sheets are covered in by a strong board having a deep circular, cut on its inner edge, used by the harpooner as a support when in the act of striking. The harpoon, or 'iron' as we whalers call it—I say we whalers on the strength of my first cruise—is made of the very best wrought iron, so tough that it will twist into any shape without breaking. It is about three and a half feet in length, with a keen, flat, barbed point at one end, and at the other a socket, in which is inserted the point of a heavy pole or staff. The whaleline is firmly fastened to the iron itself, and then connected with the staff in such a manner that, when the blow is struck and the line tightens, the staff comes out of the socket, leaving only the iron in the whale. If this plan were not adopted, the heavy pole, by its own weight and its resistance to the water, would tear out the iron, and so we should lose the fish. When in chase, the harpoon lies on the boat's head with its point over the stem ready for immediate use. Two harpoons are frequently fastened to the same line. Beneath the gunnel[8] in the bows are several brackets, containing a hatchet, knives, and a couple of lances. The whaler's lance resembles, in some measure, the harpoon—but instead of barbs, it has a fine steel blade, and is only attached to a short handline. Leather sheaths are provided for all instruments when not in use.

In the stern, or sometimes in the middle of each whale boat, is the tub. In this the line is coiled with the greatest care, as the least hitch, when it is running out, would probably turn the whole boat's crew into the water. The line—which though small is of great strength—passes along the whole length

[8] Gunnel (also, gunwale): a piece of timber around the top side of a boat, and having rowlocks (oarlocks) for the oars.

of the boat, between the rowers, and runs on a roller fixed into the stem. The rollocks,[9] in which the oars work, are muffled with rope matting. Every oar is fastened to the boat with a strong lanyard (a piece of small line), so that, when in tow of a whale, it can be tossed overboard—hanging by the lanyard—and leave all clear for the line to run out. Some boats are fitted with iron rollocks that move on a swivel; by these, the oars can be brought parallel to the boat's length, and yet remain shipped ready for use.

Each boat is usually manned by five hands and a headsman. The headsman steers during the chase, and afterwards he kills the whale, but does not 'fasten to her' with the iron. He has sole charge of the boat; and every officer of a whaler is supposed to be a headsman. Each of the boat's crew bears a particular title, thus—there are the after or stroke oarsman, the starboard and larboard midship oarsmen, and the bow oarsman or boat-steerer. The bow oarsman—who pulls the foremost oar—is harpooner, though not bearing that title, for it is unknown to South Sea whalers. He strikes the fish, and, as soon as possible, goes aft and takes the steer-oar; that is why he is called also boatsteerer. The headsman then takes his station in the bows, tends the line, and prepares to lance the whale when she rises. That is all I have to tell about the routine of a whale boat, and so now I can go on with my story.

Another boat lowered soon after we left the ship and pulled in our wake; she followed as a 'pick up boat' in case of accident. The ship—which had still a boat's crew and the idlers aboard—with yards braced sharp up, and the leech of the top-gallant sail touching, was laying a course nearly parallel to our own. The chief mate 'headed' the boat in which I rowed, and we had with us the best boatsteerer in the ship. Both were anxious to be first 'fast' to the first whale of the season. For me, it was the first whale of my life, and, though I had been rather scared by the tough yarns of the old stagers about being 'chawed up by whales,' and eaten alive by sharks, yet the active exercise and rapid motion soon stirred my blood, and I fully shared in the general

---

[9] Rollock [sic], rowlock or oarlock: a device, often U-shaped for holding an oar in place for rowing or steering.

Figure 5.7 South Sea whale fishery by E. Duncan after a painting by Garnerey, c.1820, original print from a private collection.

excitement. Three of our crew were natives of Tasmania (born of English parents), the best boatmen and the most daring whalers in the world; and, impelled by their powerful strokes, our boat was soon considerably a-head of the others. Though able to pull a good oar in a common way, I quickly found that this was very different sport to any that I had before attempted. Our tough ash oars of eighteen feet length bent and buckled with the strain. The boat sprang from each vigorous stroke, and hummed through the water as a bullet through the air. The headsman standing in the stern, with the peg of the steer-oar grasped in his left hand, stamped and raved with excitement, throwing his body forward in sympathy with each stroke, and with the right hand 'backing up' the after oar with all his strength. At the same time, he was encouraging and urging us to fresh exertions, making the most absurd promises in case of success, and threatening the boat-steerer with all sorts of awful consequences if he missed the whale. By this time we were in sight of the school, and turning my head, I could distinguish several of the low bushy spouts of the sperm whale, and catch an occasional glimpse of a huge black mass rolling in the water. But there was no time for contemplation. Another boat was creeping up to us, and we were yet some distance from the game.

The headsman grew more frantic. 'Give way, my sons! Lift her to it! Long strokes! Pile it on, my hearties! Well done, Derwenters! I've three pretty sisters you shall pick from. There she blows again! Twenty minutes more, and it's our whale.' Suddenly his face changed. 'Turned flukes!' said he. The whales had disappeared, and with peaked oars we lay motionless on the water waiting their return to the surface. In a few minutes, a short gush of steam and spray broke midway between the two boats. Half-a-dozen long strokes. 'Steady, my lads, softly, so ho! Stand up!' and the boatsteerer, peaking his oar, took his place in the bows. 'Into her! Starn all!' shouted the headsman. Both irons were buried in the whale, which lay for an instant perfectly still, whilst we backed hastily. Then the great black flukes rose into the air, and the whale 'sounded' or dived, the line running out of the tub, round the loggerhead at the stern and out at the head, with wonderful velocity. The wood smoked and cracked with the friction, and the boat's head sank under the pressure.

More than half the line was carried out before it slacked, and in the moment that it did so, we began to haul in again and coil away in the tub. But the 'struck fish' quickly appeared, the momentum acquired in rising carrying him nearly clean out of the water. He was evidently 'gallied' [frightened], making short darts in different directions; but, as the boat approached, he started off, 'eyes out,' at full speed. The line was now checked by a turn round the loggerhead, and only allowed to surge out gradually. The boat's velocity became terrific. We were carried through the water at the rate of nearly twenty miles an hour. Our little craft swept on in a deep trough; a huge wave of foam rolling a-head of us, and two green walls rising above the gunwale, threatening every moment to descend upon the boat, already half filled by the blinding spray. But, the huge animal to which our boat was harnessed soon tired of this labour, the line again slackened, and the monster lay on the surface writhing in agony, snapping his enormous jaws, and furiously lashing with his tail. As we coiled away the line, and as the distance between us and our prey decreased, I will candidly own that I was as 'gallied' as the whale itself, and would have given my own share of him to have been absent from the scene. Habit accustoms a man even to whaling; but few men, when 'fast,' for the first time, feel altogether easy. Our headsman stood coolly in the bows, lance in hand, exclaiming—'Haul me up, and he's a dead whale! A hundred barreller! Lay me on, lads!' And with the boat's nose nearly touching, he plunged a lance repeatedly into its side. 'Starn all!' The whale started ahead, but the keen weapon had reached 'the life,' and, spouting thick jets of blood, he fell into the 'flurry.' That was a tremendous spectacle. The enormous animal, convulsed in the agonies of death, rapidly circling in the midst of a dizzy whirl of blood and foam, striking alternately with head and tail; vast sheets of water flying from beneath the mighty blows, which roared like cracks of thunder. At the same time, beyond the vortex, the light boat danced as in triumph at her victory; and yet her slight frame trembled and vibrated with each stroke, as though she shuddered at the havoc she had caused.

In a short time the struggling ceased: the whale turned slowly over. We had then leisure to look about us. The two other boats were both fast to one fish, and nearly out of sight to windward. The fourth boat had struck a whale, but lost him, from the irons having drawn, and she was now making towards us. Uniting our strength we took the prize in tow, and turned our course towards the ship, eight or nine miles distant. She was making a long stretch in the direction of the fast boats. It was afternoon when, with no better dinner than dry biscuit and water, and under a burning sun, we fastened our tow line, and commenced the weary drag—the hardest, but the most welcome part of a whaler's labour. With scorched faces and blistered hands, we pulled steadily on, lightening our toil with many a chorus, and making rough calculations of the value of our prize. It was nightfall when we reached the ship, and then the whale having been firmly lashed alongside by strong chains and hawsers,[10] everything was prepared for cutting in next morning. Our shipmates soon followed with their fish, which was dropped astern, and buoyed with empty casks to prevent its sinking; for whalers not unfrequently (sic) lose the fruits of their toil by such an accident. The ship

[10] Hawser: a large rope or small cable often made of steel, by which a ship is anchored, or towed etc.

remained hove to all night, and by daylight we were hard at work. I could then have a good look at our prize.

It was a large sperm whale or cachalot, the most valuable and the most ferocious of the tribe.

The sperm whale differs considerably, both in shape and habits, from the common Greenland whale, and from the 'right whale' of the Pacific. Neither of these has teeth, but they have, instead of teeth, as is well known, a certain apparatus for procuring food. In the 'right whale,' with which only I have the pleasure of any actual acquaintance, there are attached to the whole surface of the roof of the mouth slabs of black bone, the common whalebone. These slabs, which are from five to nine feet long, twelve inches wide in the broadest part, and half an inch thick, are ranged parallel to each other on their edges, with half-inch spaces between them. From each slab hangs a narrow fringe of hair[baleen], forming a complete network. With its mouth wide open the whale rushes through the immense shoals of medusæ[11] that are found floating in the South Seas; then closing its jaws and raising the lips, the water flows out and the little red creatures ('whale feed,' sailors call them) are retained by the fringe. 'What a capital shrimp trap!' said Sir Joseph Banks. The immense tongue, which sometimes yields six or seven barrels of oil, lies on the lower jaw. It is of a glossy white, so that when the capacious mouth is open, it may be compared fancifully to a grotesque chamber with a ceiling of hair cloth and a white satin carpet.

But the sperm whale, of which I have just described the capture, has not this apparatus. Its lower jaw contains a formidable row of more than forty teeth, the jaw itself being fifteen feet long. Some of these teeth are nine inches in circumference at the base, and fit into a groove adapted to them in the upper jaw. The roof of the mouth is, in the sperm whale, covered with glistening plates of a bluish white. These plates are said to act as a bait to the fishes upon which the whale feeds, for the cachalot does not confine himself to shrimps; and, though he usually dines upon 'squid,' or cuttle-fish, of which whole acres are found floating in the Pacific, yet he does not object to a

---

[11] Medusæ: jellyfish.

dolphin or bonito,[12] and even the wary shark sometimes has the bad luck to be eaten by the great sea ogre. Our whale measured fifty-four feet in length. Of the whole bulk, the head occupied nearly a third. Round the fins and lips hung hundreds of barnacles and whale lice, and I was only deterred from pronouncing our prize ugly by the fact that he was worth some six or seven hundred pounds—a handsome sum.

Our cutting in was not delayed. Tackles were rove in the massive blocks that hung from the fore and main-mast heads; others were suspended from the yards and spans; and strong purchases were prepared to cant the whale, so as to get the blubber from his back and sides. The head was cut off and dropped astern for a while, until the carcase was disposed of, though this is an unusual mode of cutting in, and only practised in some ships. Strips of blubber, called 'blanket pieces,' were cut along the whole length of the fish. A wooden toggle having been passed through one end of the strip and a block hooped to it, the men in-board hoisted away, those on the whale loosening the mass with their blubber spades. Other toggles were inserted to form fresh supports; and when the blanket piece had been thus hoisted in, it was passed into the blubber-room—a square apartment under the main hatch. Some of these blanket pieces will weigh thirty or forty hundred weight. In the blubber room they were cut into 'horse pieces' more than a foot square, and piled in heaps, from which the blood and oil flowed out in streams. As the strips were cut off, the whale was canted, or turned, by the tackles until every morsel of fat had been stripped from the carcase.

While we were thus occupied, sea birds in thousands gathered round the ship. The sea was covered with fatty matter and white patches of spermaceti,[13] and from beneath us, shoals of sharks darted up at their dead enemy, tearing off large pieces of his flesh. The sharks prefer 'whale beef' to a tough bony man.

---

[12] Bonito: fish of the mackerel family.

[13] Spermaceti: a white crystalline waxy solid that separates from sperm oil, especially from the head cavities. It was used chiefly in candles, ointments and cosmetics.

The fins having been cut off, and the body of the whale clean picked, it was turned adrift, and, deprived of the light blubber, sank immediately. The 'case,' or head, was next brought alongside, the lower jaw being uppermost. This was separated from the case and hoisted on deck. The bony palate or upper jaw was then raised, and from beneath it was cut the 'junk,' an enormous mass of blubber, weighing some thousands of pounds. We had then reached the real case, in which is secreted the most valuable product of the sperm whale. Strong tackles hoisted it above the wash of the waves, and a hole was broken into it, through which buckets were let down and whipped on deck filled with the precious liquor. This was pure spermaceti: whalers call it 'head-matter.' When first extracted, it is a clear liquid slightly tinged with pink; but, on being exposed to the air it coagulates and solidifies. The oil with which it is mixed is expelled by pressure, and the spermaceti remains in hard masses of thin irregular flakes. The oil thus procured is the finest and purest of all animal oils, and burns with a peculiarly bright clear flame.

One of the men presently stepped into the case, and proceeded to knock down the partitions which divide it into several small apartments, each filled with head-matter. The whole space was thus turned into a large room.

The blubber having been separated from the 'white horse' of the junk, all the remainder of the carcase was turned over to the sharks. 'White horse' is a term sometimes applied to all the useless flesh of the whale, but more particularly to a mass of whitish stringy gristle, which covers the head, and seems to serve the purpose of a 'cork fender' in defending it from blows.

The 'try-works' were then in full play. They are three iron pots, firmly bedded in brick-work, amidships, with fire-places beneath them, separated from the deck by a pen filled with water. Into these pots a barrel of oil was poured from the case (which yields from twelve to twenty barrels), and the fires lighted. The 'horse-pieces' were pitched upon deck from the blubber-room with a long fork, and carried to the 'mincing horses'—small blocks or tables securely fastened to the deck. A boy holding a horsepiece on the block by a small hook, a man with a two-handled knife—resembling a joiner's drawing-knife turned upside down—rapidly cut it into thin slices, which just hung together. It was then a 'book,' ready for melting, or 'trying out.' The pots were well filled with books, and as the oil rose to the surface it was skimmed off with a large ladle, and poured into a copper cooler, from whence it was transferred to casks, and safely stowed in the hold. Whalers require very little fuel, as the scraps that remain from the melted blubber are enough to keep the fires going.

A whale ship presents a strange scene during the process of trying out. The decks are literally swimming in oil; it covers the ropes, the men's clothes; the very galley and cooking coppers are saturated with it, and every mouthful of beef and biscuit has the whale flavour. The white sails are blackened by the smoke, and the neat trim ship of yesterday has suddenly become a floating mass of dirt and grease enveloped in thick, black, and stinking clouds. Our sails were nearly all furled at sundown, but the work went on all night. The fires threw a red glare on the ropes and spars, and, fed by the oily scraps, sprang up in vivid flames that lightened all the sea. Dark figures moved in the red gleam, armed with strange weapons, or stood beside great cauldrons, slowly stirring round their boiling broth. Unearthly noises and wild songs mingled with the low dash of the sea, the mournful creaking of the spars, and the sad moaning of the tainted wind; whilst over all hung a thick canopy of heavy smoke which, in that calm weather, drooped around the ship, and formed a fitting veil for such a dismal spectacle.

But, to the actors in it the scene had nothing of dismalness, for out of all this smoke and dirt, we were to get clean gold. We were sea alchemists. Every man in a whale ship shares in the profits of the voyage, his wages being paid by the 'lay.' A certain share is appropriated by the owners of the ship, and the remainder is divided among the crew; the lay of a foremast hand, a common 'spouter,' being about a sixty-fifth in a colonial whaler. The value of both oil and bone is fixed before the ship sails, so that the markets have no effect on the 'lay;' but the price thus fixed is always far below the actual value of the articles.

Few vessels are now fitted out in England for the South Sea fisheries; nearly all the British ships in the trade belong to Australian ports; their oil is discharged at the Antipodes, and then re-shipped for London. Colonial whalers usually remain at sea six months, taking sperm whales when they can catch them, and filling up with black oil from the 'right whale.' But the trade is chiefly engrossed by the Americans, who have always a numerous fleet employed in it. At some seasons it is almost impossible to enter a port on the west coast of South America, in the South Sea Islands, or New Holland without finding a 'Yankee spouter' refitting or refreshing. The number of American whalers has ranged, for some years, between six and seven hundred; but the increasing scarcity of fish has latterly decreased their number. The additional expense incurred, in consequence of the length of time which it now takes to fill a ship, has rendered whaling a less profitable business than it used to be. The American vessels are usually fitted for a four years' voyage, and often remain that time at sea.

13
Chip: The Treasures of the Deep
Samuel Sidney

Numbers of whales.
Volume: 2 Number: 30 Pages: 94–95
Date: October 19, 1850
Fee: 5 shillings for ½ Column.

Some of these treasures were fished up, and brought to our readers' knowledge in our article on Billingsgate in our tenth number. We received an additional illustration of the subject from a correspondent:—'People talk of the 'treasures of the deep' with generally a very confused notion of their own meaning, if, indeed, they have any meaning at all. Probably they have some incoherent ideas of rich merchantmen that have gone down with their costly cargoes, mingled with coral reefs and pearl fisheries, as forming no inconsiderable portion of those treasures. But how often do they think of the countless riches which the sea produces in the living things that dwell in it? Take, for illustration, the whale alone. For ten days the writer of this was becalmed in the latitude of the Azores or Western Isles. During the whole of that period huge whales were incessantly 'blowing' in every direction round the ship. As many as twenty or thirty at a time might be seen rolling their unwieldy bodies half out of the sea, and puffing up large fountains of spray into the air. At a moderate calculation, two hundred and fifty whales were seen from the deck in those ten days. At an equally moderate calculation, each whale was worth four hundred pounds. Their gross value was, therefore, one hundred thousand pounds!'

Contributors to *Household Words*

The following biographical notes have quoted extensively from:
Anne Lohrli, *Household Words: A Weekly Journal 1850–1859, Conducted by Charles Dickens*, Toronto: University of Toronto Press, 1973. (Reprinted by permission, University of Toronto Press)

Other sources include:
Peter Ackroyd, *Dickens*, London: Mandarin Paperbacks, 1991.
Australian Dictionary of Biography 1851–1890, Vols. 1, 4 & 5, various eds., Melbourne: Melbourne University Press, 1959–76.
Tim Flannery, *The Birth of Melbourne*, Melbourne: Text Publishing, 2004
John Forster, *The Life of Charles Dickens: The Fireside Dickens*, London: Chapman and Hall Ltd. and Henry Frowde, c.1874.
Harry Gordon, *An Eyewitness History of Australia*, Melbourne: John Currey O'Neil, pp. 55–61, 1986.
Nancy Keesing, (Ed.), *History of the Australian Gold Rushes: By Those Who Were There*, Sydney: Angus & Robertson, Australia, 1987.
Mary Lazarus, *A Tale of Two Brothers: Charles Dickens's Sons in Australia*, Sydney: Angus & Robertson, 1973.
Una Pope-Hennessy, *Charles Dickens, 1812–1870*, London: The Reprint Society, 1947.
Harry Stone, *Charles Dickens' Uncollected Writings from Household Words 1850–1859*, Vols. 1 & 2, Bloomington, Indiana: University of Indiana Press, 1968.

Each entry finishes with the title(s) included in these volumes, with the volume number in parentheses; (1) *Convict Stories*, (2) *Immigration*, (3) *Frontier Stories*, (4) *Mining and Gold*, (5) *Maritime Conditions*.

Anonymous, payment for the item listed below (*H.W.* Office Book) was made to Robert Bell an intimate friend of Dickens. Bell had provided to the editorial office a letter written to him from a friend in Australia. It was dated 25 December 1850 and from North Kapunda, South Australia.[1]
– 'Life in the Burra Mines of South Australia' (4).

Anonymous (no payment recorded). In the article the contributor explains how two persons, 'fighting fire with fire' can, 'with perfect ease,' contain and control a bush fire.
– 'Chip: The Bush-Fire Extinguisher', W.H. Wills & a correspondent (3).

Capper, John (1814–1898). Capper was a resident of Ceylon (Sri Lanka) who worked as a journalist covering events in Ceylon and India for forty years. He was a correspondent for the London *Times* and also a regular contributor to *H.W.* Nearly sixty of his articles were published in *H.W.* between March 1851 and March, 1858.

Capper was the author of many books on Australia: *Perils, Pastimes, and Pleasures of an Emigrant in Australia*; *The Emigrants' Guide to Australia*, 1852; and also, *Australia: As a Field for Capital, Skill, and Labour*, 1854. In addition, he recorded himself on the title pages of two of his books as the author of 'Our Gold Colonies' and on the title page of another, as author of the 'Gold Fields'.
– 'Off to the Diggings!' (5); 'First Stage to Australia', Capper & W.H. Wills (2); 'The Great Screw' [Screw Propeller] (5).

Chisholm, Caroline (1808–1877) was born in England. From 1832 to 1838 her husband, Captain Archibald, was stationed in Madras. It was there she began a lifelong career as a passionate social activist establishing a school for the neglected children of soldiers.

She came to Australia on leave in 1836, and remained in Sydney after her husband's recall to active service (1840–45), to continue her work protecting poor working women. She established the Female Emigrants' Home in Sydney in 1841 and conducted groups of immigrant women into the interior. This was done both to safeguard them and to find them suitable situations.

She met every immigrant ship, and as a result, founded the Registry Office for Immigrant Families. While in Australia she published *Female Immigration Considered* (1842), describing her activities in the Female Emigrants' Home.

After her husband's retirement in 1845 he joined her in collecting information from over 600 immigrants about their experiences in Australia. This was later to serve as a guide for future immigrants. On their return to England (1846–54), the Chisholm's worked to assist immigrants and helped the wives and children of liberated convicts, then in Australia, to migrate to join their husbands. In 1849 she established The Family Colonization Loan Society to enable the poor to migrate to Australia. Chisholm wrote pamphlets on immigration and wrote letters to influential persons seeking assistance for her projects, as well as supervising the passage of immigrant ships.[2]

On 24 February 1850, Elizabeth Herbert, the wife of Dickens' friend Sydney Herbert (who financially supported both Chisholm's and Dickens' humanitarian work), wrote to Mrs Chisholm:

> I saw Mr. Dickens to-day and he has commissioned me to say that if you will allow him, and unless he hears to the contrary from you, he will call upon you at 2 o'clock on Tuesday next, the 26th … I told him about your emigrants' letter, and he seemed to think that giving them publicity would be an important engine towards helping in our work, and he has so completely the confidence of the lower classes (who all read his Books if they can read at all) that I think if you can persuade him to bring them out in his new work it will be an immense step gained.[3]

This timely meeting of Chisholm with Dickens seems to have influenced his attitude to Australia—well beyond the articles published in her name. Her 'emigrants' letters' appeared in the first number of Dickens' 'new work'. When writing to Wills on March 6, 1850, Dickens mentioned 'A Bundle of Emigrants' Letters' as 'a little article of my own … introducing five or six originals [letters], which are extremely good. Dickens paid tribute to, and endorsed, Mrs Chisholm's work[4] thus providing powerful aid, publicity and credibility to her work.

When her husband returned to Australia in 1851 to continue their work, she remained in England until 1854. It was during this time that amendments to the Passenger Act (1852) to improve conditions aboard migrant ships took effect. The new regulations were largely due to the Chisholms' advocacy.

Six articles written for *H.W.* from 1850 to 1852 promoted her work. Two were by W.H. Wills, 'Safety for Female Emigrants' and 'Official Emigration'. The others were by Samuel Sidney, 'Two Scenes of the Life of John Bodger', 'Three Colonial Epochs', 'Better Ties than Red Tape' and 'What to Take to Australia'. Sidney also referred to Mrs Chisholm's work in his book *Emigrant's Journal.*

After returning to Australia (1854) she toured the goldfields to assess conditions for travellers and this resulted in ten shelter sheds being built on the routes to the diggings. She lobbied government to assist settlers to gain small land holdings and reform land administration.[5] The Chisholms returned to England in 1866. In recognition of her service to immigrants her portrait was placed on the first issued series of the Australian five-dollar note (1966).

– 'A Bundle of Emigrants' Letters', Charles Dickens & Caroline Chisholm (2); 'Pictures of Life in Australia', Charles Dickens & Caroline Chisholm (2).

Cox, Miss (no first name recorded) whose address was noted as Kensington. The article 'Easy Spelling and Hard Reading' reproduces the letter of a barely literate Englishman who had emmigrated to Australia. W.H. Wills (*H.W.* editor, see below) was probably responsible for the introductory comments in the article which criticised the 'want of national means of education' in England, as a result the son of poor parents grew up without the schooling that would make him 'a literate and useful citizen'. This was one of many articles on education published in *H.W.* decrying the lack of education for the masses.

– 'Chip: Easy Spelling and Hard Reading', Miss Cox & W.H. Wills (2).

Dickens, Charles (1812–1870). Journalist, editor, novelist and accomplished stage performer. He wrote fourteen novels. As a boy Dickens worked for five months in a blacking factory while his family was in debtor's prison. This experience had a powerful influence on his thinking for the remainder of his life. His writing career started when he was employed as an office boy in an attorney's office. After learning shorthand Dickens became an expert parliamentary and court reporter, as well as general reporter of the *Mirror of Parliament*; *True Sun* and the *Morning Chronicle*. As a young man he contributed sketches to *Monthly Chronicle*; *Evening Chronicle* and *Bell's Life in London*.

Throughout his highly productive career Dickens was primarily a journalist, always seeking to promote social change and awareness. He established several publications: *Daily News* (1846); *Household Words* (1850–1859); and *All the Year Round* (1859–1870). In January 1850, two months before *H.W.* was first published Dickens began *Household Narrative of Current Events*. It was a monthly supplement of news[6] supplying condensed reports of proceedings in parliament as well as chronicling the principal lawsuits and articles on important books. There were no editorial or other comments. It also included statistics on crime, accidents and disasters, social, sanitary and municipal progress, obituaries, colonies and dependencies, foreign events, literature and arts, commercial records, stocks and share, and emigration figures.

Dickens seems to have had a fascination with Australia. According to his friend and biographer John Forster, during the 1850s he had a 'recurring notion' about emigrating,[7] (which was more likely a fantasy than a serious consideration). Even so, in 1862 he did seriously contemplate a trip to Australia when offered £10,000 to perform his readings,[8] (and this provides an indication of his popularity in Australia).

Two of Dickens' children migrated to Australia. Alfred (1845–1912) arrived in 1865, receiving assistance from Sir Archibald Michie (see below). He became a stock and station agent in the Western Districts of Victoria before moving to Melbourne in 1882. Alfred returned to England in 1910. Edward (1852–1905) came to Australia at the age of sixteen (in 1869) and lived in Western NSW for over thirty years. For a time he owned a station near Bourke, later working at the Lands Office in Moree and briefly represented Wilcannia in the NSW Legislative Assembly. Dickens maintained a correspondence with his sons in Australia until his death in 1870.[9]

Dickens wrote or co-wrote nearly 200 articles for *H.W.* including prose and verse, as well as novels printed in instalments, such as *Hard Times*. He received £500 per annum for his work on *H.W.* plus a share of the profits.
– 'A Bundle of Emigrants' Letters', Charles Dickens & Mrs Chisholm (2); 'Pictures of Life in Australia', Charles Dickens & Mrs Chisholm (2); 'Chip: Fine Art in Australia' (2); 'Home for Homeless Women' (2).

Fawkner, John Pascoe (1792–1869) a correspondent and pioneer settler in Australia, especially of Melbourne. Born in London, Fawkner had received only a few years schooling. His father was sentenced to transportation but was permitted to take his family with him when dispatched from England in April 1803. Until October 1835, John Fawkner had various occupations, mainly in Van Diemen's Land, from where he arranged an expedition to Port Phillip for the purpose of establishing a farm on the northern side of the Yarra (with 500 sheep and fifty cattle). The settlement ultimately became Melbourne.

In 1838 Fawkner founded the *Melbourne Advertiser*, the first newspaper in Victoria, followed by the *Port Phillip Patriot*. He took an active role in matters relating to governing Victoria, both before and after separation from NSW in 1851. Fawkner held various official posts and served in the Victorian legislature for eighteen years.

Fawkner's pioneering work in Port Phillip received mention in *H.W.* in Howitt's 'The Old and New Squatter', 8 December, 1855. The article published in *H.W.* entitled 'A Colonial Patriot' was a letter to Dickens from Fawkner and not intended for publication. In the letter he wrote: 'I pray you to pardon this liberty, but I could not refrain from thanking you for the very favourable manner in which my conduct has been reported in your journal'. He stated that he had almost all of Dickens' work as well as *H.W.* and Dickens' monthly periodical, *Household Narrative of Current Events*.[10]
– 'Chip: A Colonial Patriot', Fawkner & Howitt (3).

Gill, Charles (contributor not identified). The introduction to the item states that the 'contributor is an Englishman for six years resident in Victoria.' Gill's article discusses the climate of Victoria and also contains a reference to the huge bush fire of 1851, 'already described in this Journal' (Black Thursday, of May 10, 1856 written by William Howitt).
– 'Sultry December' (2).

Gwynne, Francis squatter and landowner in NSW who migrated to Australia (date uncertain). In partnership with his brothers Richard and Henry, Francis took up Crown Lands outside the 'Limits of Location'. The Gwynne brothers were recorded as being the holders of the Barratta cattle station, north of the Edward River, in the Murrumbidgee squatting district, which they held until 1853. Henry then took over Werai station and Francis bought Murgah station, adjoining Barratta to the west, with 750 cattle for £6750, which he sold in 1872. In the 1860s he was a JP in the Moulamein district.[11]

The two letters that constitute the article were addressed by the writer to 'a relative in Cheshire,' apparently another brother, William. Gwynne's letter records raids by 'blacks' on the Gwynne's cattle and attacks on the Gwynne's two stations. *H.W.* published the letters to 'furnish some idea of how new localities are colonised by such enterprising pioneers as the writer.'
– 'Two Letters from Australia', Francis Gwynne & W.H. Wills (3)

Hill, Catherine (correspondent not identified). Hill was referred to in an editorial comment as a 'correspondent in Adelaide, Australia.'
– 'Chip: Hornet Architecture', (2).

Hogarth, Jr (identity uncertain), thought to be a son of George Hogarth who was part of Dickens' circle of friends and is recorded as having had five sons and five daughters. George Hogarth was a lawyer, music critic and journalist who contributed four articles to *Household Words.*

Little is known about the contributor of the articles listed below. The details that accompanied them, (which are unconfirmed) stated that the contributor had migrated to Australia before the goldrush at 'the beginning of the winter of 1850 and was working quietly in Sydney, [and] by no means dissatisfied with his position.' When rumours of Bathurst gold reached the city, Hogarth resigned his position and advertised in the *Sydney Morning Herald* for 'a gentleman, willing to join him and share the expenses of going to Turon diggings.' He chose as partner one of the men who answered his advertisement and proceeded with him to the diggings. He was there (unsuccessfully) for about four months (see, 'Cradle and the Grave').[12]

Hogarth co-authored two articles for *Household Words*—one in conjunction with Richard Horne and another with Joseph Morley (see biographies below).

- 'Chip: Look Before You Leap', R.H. Horne & Hogarth Jr (2); 'The Cradle and the Grave', Hogarth Jr. & Morley (presumably, Joseph) (2)

Horne, Richard Henry (or Hengist) (1802–1884), was a London-born author who was educated at Sandhurst. He had a life full of adventure which included 'a tour in the Mexican navy, pitched battles, an encounter with a shark, yellow fever, shipwreck, mutiny, and fire at sea; as well as exploits with Indians in the U.S.A.' He produced poems, plays, travel narratives, novels, biographies, children's stories and various articles on a huge range of subjects. Horne met Dickens in the 1830s and they became good friends with much in common. In 1841 Horne served on royal commission on child employment in factories.[13]

From the commencement of publication of *H. W.* in 1850, Horne was one of the early salaried members of the staff receiving £250 per annum, (half the rate of Dickens' own salary). He wrote original prose and poetry, revised contributed articles, and assisted Wills in editing the journal.

Horne travelled to Australia (arriving in September 1852) in the company of William Howitt, having agreed to supply *H.W.* with a number of travel pieces in return for advances to equip the expedition and for regular payments to his wife.[14]

Horne remained in Australia for seventeen years, returning to England in 1869. While in Australia he had a varied career. He became commander of a private gold escort and in 1853, assistant gold commissioner at Heathcote and Waranga until 1854.[15] He was employed as a clerk for Sir Archibald Michie (see below) a commissioner of sewerage and water, as well as standing unsuccessfully for a seat in parliament in 1857. Horne was an active member of Melbourne's Garrick Club. He wrote a satirical piece about the club whose members went on to perform it.[16] On his return to England in 1869, Dickens refused to have anything to do with him because he had contributed little to Mrs Horne's support during his time in Australia.

He wrote sixty-nine articles for *H.W.* (twelve of which related to Australia) and twenty-four poems. During his career he published many books of prose and poetry, including a book for potential migrants, *Australian Facts and Prospects*, London, 1859. In 1874 Horne was granted a pension of £50 per annum in recognition of his services to literature.

– 'Pictures of Life in Australia', Caroline Chisholm & Horne (2); 'A Digger's Diary', [in 4 parts] (4); 'Chip: Look Before You Leap', Horne & Hogarth Jr. (2); 'Gentlemen and Bullocks' (3); 'Canvass Town [sic]' (2); 'Chip: Digging Sailors' (4); 'Chip: A Digger's Wedding' (4); 'Convicts in the Gold Region' (1)

Howitt, William (1792–1879) received his education at a Quaker school. He was self-taught in languages, chemistry, botany, natural science and dispensing of medicines. He became writer and is credited with 180 publications. Along with his wife Mary (who contributed three prose articles and seven items of verse) he was a regular contributor to *Household Words*. The Howitts were great admirers of Dickens' writings, particularly because of the couple's social awareness and advocacy for reform.

Due to financial need, at the age of sixty, William Howitt sailed to Australia in the company of Richard Horne, along with Howitt's two sons—Alfred William (known as William, 1830–1909) and Charlton. Howitt's younger brothers Godfrey (1800–1873) a physician and natural scientist and Richard (1799–1870) a poet, had preceded them to Port Phillip in 1840.

When Howitt arrived in Melbourne he already had a reputation as an author and poet. While in Australia he wrote many articles describing in detail aspects of life and work at the diggings.[17] His accounts were acknowledged for their 'objectivity and tolerance'.[18]

Howitt travelled to the goldfields with his sons at intervals during the two years and discovered the rich Nine-Mile-Creek diggings, where he was moderately successful.[19] He was said to have revelled in bush life and the strange flora and fauna. He recognised the necessity to reform the land laws and also offered sensible suggestions for improvement in the gold commissioners 'comic opera' police force. His advice was ignored. Howitt returned to England in 1854.

His son Alfred William elected to stay in Australia where he initially farmed at his uncle's farm in Caulfield, and later had interests were pastoral stations at Yea and Cape Schanck.[20] His brother Charlton went to New Zealand in 1860 where he worked as a surveyor. Alfred William was to become a leading explorer and led a party to find and later retrieve the remains of Burke and Wills. He was a natural scientist and pioneer and an authority on Aboriginal culture and social organisation. He was acknowledged by Sir Baldwin Spencer for laying down the foundations of the scientific study of Aborigines. He became a drover, police magistrate, goldfields warden and secretary for mines. Alfred William was a prolific writer, especially about the Victorian goldfields.[21]

It is reasonable to assume that Howitt maintained a correspondence with his sons long after his return to England, thus keeping him, and his circle, informed about current events in Australia.

Other publications by William Howitt include: *A Boys Adventure in the Wilds of Australia*, 1854; *Land Labour and Gold, or Two Years in Victoria*, (London: Longmans, 1855); *Tasmania and New Zealand*, 1856. His articles in the book were published first in *Household Words* and later reproduced as interpolated stories in *Tallangetta: the Squatter's Home*, (by William Howitt). Two Vols, London: Longman, Brown, Green, Longmans and Roberts, 1857 (publication in *H. W.* acknowledged).[22]
– 'The Old and New Squatter' (3); 'The Landlord' (3); 'Black Thursday' (3); 'Gold Hunting in Two Parts' (4); 'The Land Shark' (3)

Irwin, Mr (not identified) In the item below, Irwin mentions having been to Norfolk Island. He wrote, 'I know the place well and the people living there, convicts and all. How I came by my knowledge is a question which I am not obliged to answer; but, for the comfort of the clean-fingered, I am not legally pitch.' A further article, 'Caught in a Typhoon', was published in *H. W.* in 1853, where Irwin recounted a stormy passage on board ship from Macau to Singapore.[23] He wrote two further articles about Australia in 1853 and 1854.

In the *Geelong Advertiser* in December 1854 there was an item covering the Eureka Stockade by a Samuel Irwin, who was 'regarded as one of the most responsible eyewitnesses and his very full and accurate report of the incident,'[24] some of which was used in government dispatches to the Secretary for the Colony about the affair. During the same period he is recorded as being the editor of the *Ballarat Star*. Whether Mr Irwin (above) and Samuel Irwin were the same person has not been confirmed.

– 'Norfolk Island', Irwin & Henry Morley (1); 'Chip: Sentimental Geography' (5); 'Chip: The Antecedents of Australia' (1).

Keene, William Thomas (1798–1872). William Keene's brothers, John and James (of Kingsmead Street, Bath), were commercial printers and proprietors of *Keene's Bath Journal*, founded 1744.[25] The *Sydney Morning Herald*'s and additional information supporting the article was supplied to Wills (Dickens editor) by one of William's brothers.

William Keene emmigrated to Victoria in the early 1850's later moving with his family to NSW. He had studied medicine in London, and later geology and engineering, working as a mining engineer and civil engineer in Bordeaux France in the 1830's. Keene completed a geological survey of the Fitzroy iron mines near Mittagong, and in 1854 was appointed Examiner of Coalfields. He remained principally in NSW and in the 1860's worked on the coal-bearing rocks and oil shale in the Sydney Basin.

His geological reports were published principally in government gazettes and some in newspapers. He is remembered for his work on coal deposits and the water supply of the area, and for providing geological material for exhibition in London, Paris and Melbourne as well as to collectors around the world. William Keene was a member of the Geological Society of London where he published two articles in *Quarterly Journal*.[26] He also served as a magistrate for a short time.

– 'Chip: A Golden Newspaper', William Keene & William Wills (4).

Lang, John (1816–1864) barrister, journalist, novelist. He was born in Parramatta, NSW the son of Walter Lang, a merchant adventurer who married Elizabeth Harris, the Australian born daughter of First Fleeter John Harris. Lang was educated at Sydney College and Trinity College Cambridge. He studied law and was called to the bar in 1838 and in 1839 returned to Sydney. In 1843 he left Sydney for Calcutta where he lived for most of the remainder of his life. In India, Lang founded and edited the newspaper *The Moffussilite*, and later, for a time edited the *Optimist* in Meerut. He devoted most of his time to literary works while contributing to several publications. Lang wrote twenty novels, most of which were published anonymously in *The Moffussilite.*

John Lang published several books relating to Australia including *The Forger's Wife*, which is almost identical to his 'Charles Fredrick Howard', a story in *Legends of Australia*, (1842) which he published anonymously. He also published *Botany Bay: or True Tales of Early Australia* (1859), a collection of short sketches and stories (thinly disguised as fiction) of events and people in the convict period.[27] Lang's books were very popular.

He wrote twenty-four articles for *H.W.* the ones listed below, together with five additional stories were later published as *Botany Bay*, by John Lang, Esq., Barrister at Law, London: William Tegg, 1859, (publication in *H.W.* acknowledged). *Botany Bay* was frequently reprinted. These included *Clever Criminals* and *Remarkable Convicts.* A Melbourne edition (reprinting only ten of the thirteen stories that constituted the book) was titled *Fisher's Ghost and Other Stories of the Early Days of Australia.*[28]
– 'Fisher's Ghost' (3); 'Tracks in the Bush' (3); 'An Illustrious British Exile' (1); 'A Special Convict' (1); 'Baron Wald' (1); 'Three Celebrities' (1); 'Kate Crawford' (1); 'Miss Saint Felix' (1).

Macpherson, Ossian (contributor not identified) published four articles in *Household Words.* Three printed in 1851 dealt with the writer's interest in improving social conditions and redressing common social abuses. 'The Smithfield Model' concerns the removal of the filthy, unhygienic Smithfield cattle market from the centre of the City of London (and other towns and cities). 'A Few Facts about Salt' denounces the 'odious imposition' of government tax on Indian salt and the injustice done to the natives. 'Excursion Trains' calls for railway companies to institute cheap fares for patrons by showing the benefit to the owners themselves.[29]

The fourth article on Australia, written in 1852, in conjunction with Morley and Mulock in this collection, is titled 'The Harvest of Gold', is attributed to the same author. Although not dealing specifically with social need, it relates the history of the discovery of gold in Australia and detailed conditions in the goldfields as recorded in newspapers and also, in letters from immigrants such as Mulock (see below). It also discusses the economic effects on Britain should a decrease in the value of gold occur as a result of finding it in Australia. The discussion about the decrease in the value of gold was probably the writing of Morley (see below), who dealt with that matter in an article in the following month.
- 'The Harvest of Gold' (4).

Marryatt, Miss (contributor uncertain). Frederick Marryatt was a friend of Dickens. They met socially and sometimes corresponded with each other. His daughters were all writers. Two, Augusta and Emilia wrote stories with Australia as a setting. 'Friends in Australia' is about an Englishman who takes a voyage to Australia for the sake of his health. The story records a horseback trip in New South Wales, and some incidents, 'for the most part true,' related by the Englishman's friend of his experiences in Australia 'twenty years ago, less or more.' There is no suggestion that the writer had any personal experience of Australia.
- 'Friends in Australia' (3).

Meredith, Louisa Anne (Twarmley) (1812–1895) was born near Birmingham. She published poems and at least twenty-three books, many with illustrations that she had designed and etched herself. Louisa was fearless as an author; she wrote on social and religious issues, and published several newspaper articles in support of Chartists.[30] In 1839 she married Charles Meredith, a squatter from New South Wales and, in the same year, accompanied him to Sydney, and later to Tasmania, where she remained for the rest of her life. For the fifty years she lived in Australia, Meredith recorded colonial life in NSW, Victoria and Tasmania.

She became interested in politics, and wrote unsigned articles for Tasmanian newspapers and contributed to *Australian Ladies' Annual*, in addition to sending occasional articles to British periodicals, including *HouseholdWords*. Meredith wrote seventeen books, including *Notes and Sketches of New South Wales* (1844). At least nine of her books written in either prose form or poetry, related to Tasmania and many were illustrated. She was passionate about the protection of native wildlife and wrote many books describing Tasmanian flowers and insects, with the descriptions interspersed with verses and illustrated colour plates from her drawings. These included *Some of My Bush Friends in Australia* (1860) and a second series of *Bush Friends* which were published in 1891. She also wrote *Tasmanian Friends and Foes; Feathered, Furred and Finned* (in story form); *Grandmamma's Verse Book for Young Australia*; and, *Waratah Rhymes for Young Australia* and other books.[31]

After her husband's death in 1880 Meredith was granted a pension of £100 per annum by the Tasmanian government in recognition to her work in literature, art and science.[32]
– 'The Shadows of the Golden Image' (4); 'Little Bell' (3).

Michie, Sir Archibald (1810–1899), English born jurist and statesman. He studied law and was called to the bar in 1838 and also worked as a journalist for the *Atlas* newspaper.

He migrated to Sydney in 1839 to practise law and in May 1841 was admitted to the NSW Barrister Roll. He sailed to South Australia in 1847 and in the same year a publication containing a two page preface by Michie, about the *Case of Mr. W.H. Barber …* (a convicted convict, later established as innocent), was printed.[33] Following his return to Sydney from South Australia, Michie was endorsed by the Anti-Transportation League for the Legislative Council seat of Cumberland County in 1849, but was unsuccessful.

He then returned to England arriving soon after W. H. Barber, (himself a lawyer and now pardoned) had published a book about his case. Barber's book and Michie's arrival in England coincided with the publication of *Household Words* and it is likely that this is when the articles listed below were written. Dickens was interested in the issue of Barber as he had a copy of Barbers book in his library.[34] In July and August of this same year Dickens published Barber's story in *H.W.* as 'Transported for Life: In Two Parts', (reprinted in Book 1) with Barber's name withheld. These articles were written by William Thomas (see biography below).

About 1852 Michie left England for Canada, then proceeded to Sydney and finally settled in Melbourne where he practised law. He was admitted to serve in the Victorian Supreme Court and later (1863) became Victoria's first QC. In 1856 he was elected to the new Victorian Legislative Council. He was twice attorney-general and was minister for justice and later, for six years, agent-general for Victoria in London. He was made a K.C.M.G., and returned to Melbourne on his retirement. He was regarded as having a brilliant legal mind and is remembered as one of the barristers who defended the Eureka Rebels (1855).[35]

It is highly probable Michie met Dickens while in England and it is known that Dickens corresponded with him in Australia. One of Dickens' letters referred to *H.W.* writer Richard Horne (see above) whom Michie had employed as a clerk in his office. Dickens recalled seeing Horne invent 'an immense corkscrew,' before he left England; it was to be used for the 'infallible' extraction of gold with which he expected to make his fortune at the diggings.[36] In contrast, when Dickens wrote to Horne about Michie (1865), he declared his 'appreciation of Michie's kindness to young Alfred Dickens, who had migrated to Australia in May of that year.'[37]

Michie was a distinguished speaker and lecturer, and several of his addresses were published as pamphlets. He wrote for *Melbourne Herald*, *Punch* and for many years was the Victorian correspondent for *The Times*.[38]

Michie's name did not appear in items listed below. In the first, (written in conjunction with Morley) the writer identified himself as one of the 'London barristers' in Sydney and states that his 'own diggings' were in the Supreme Court. He records a trip to Maitland related to the assize held there.

He describes Sydney as he saw the city on his first arrival and as he came to know it, 'a subsequent nine years' experience.'[39]
– 'Going Circuit at the Antipodes', Michie & Morley (1); 'Chip: A Visit to the Burra Burra Mines' (4).

Morley, Henry (1822–1892), the archetypical 'Man of Letters' was educated in England at King's College, London, in the faculty of arts and medicine and also in Germany. He practised medicine for four years and then for two years conducted his own school. From 1851 to 1865 Morley served on the staff of *H.W.* and *All the Year Round.* He was appointed professor of English language and literature at University College from 1865 to 1889 and held other academic appointments.

Morley's friendship with Dickens developed through his involvement with *H.W.* Lohrli records that 'in a letter of 1850, Morley expressed great admiration for Dickens' writing; opining that Dickens lacked 'sound literary taste ... his own genius, brilliant as it is, appears often in a dress which shows that he has more heart and wit than critical refinement'; a conviction that was to remain long after Dickens' death.[40] Also that Morley's connection to *H.W.* resulted from Dickens' interest in certain papers on sanitation and health that he had written. Two of the papers, published in *Journal of Public Health*, had been reprinted in newspapers. Dickens' request that Morley might write for *H.W.* on matters of sanitation was enclosed in a letter from Forster, a lawyer, and close friend of Dickens.

Initially Morley was not enthusiastic about writing for *H.W.* because the audience he would be writing for was distinctly low-brow—as according to him, his usual audience in comparison was 'clever, liberal-minded and loved wit'. However he agreed to do so. Morley wrote, 'but for the sake of making Dickens' acquaintance ... and having 'a second pulpit to preach health'. Initially he found it difficult to find the right style to communicate with his new audience. He wrote on many topics, especially those related to health, including sanitation, medicine and scientific matters, conditions in factories (that drew the wrath of factory-owners), life on board ships, mines, schooling and other social conditions. Some of his articles were rejected by Dickens, some rewritten and others returned for revision.[41]

In 1851 Morley was offered a salaried position on *H.W.* at £5 per week and was the only university-educated staff member. In that capacity, to use his own words, 'to act as a sort of deputy-lieutenant, writing papers of my own, revising or rewriting any paper found in the letter-box that contained matter useful to the public, that was ill-written or ill-arranged, and making myself generally useful'.

Morley wrote 382 prose article and five poems for *Household Words*. Four of his poems were reprinted in *Gossip*. He also contributed articles to many literary journals. He was the author of books of poems, fairy tales, numerous biographies, as well as ten volumes on English writers. In the latter part of his life, he edited some 300 volumes of English and foreign classics. Morley wrote, or co-wrote twelve articles for *H.W.*, that related to Australia, (listed below) and co-wrote one relating to New Zealand.

– 'Going Circuit at the Antipodes', Michie & Morley (1); 'A Rainy Day on the 'Euphrates'' (2); 'Norfolk Island', Irwin & Morley (1); 'The Harvest of Gold' Morley, Macpherson & Mulock (4); 'Chip: Highland Emigration' (2); 'Sailors' Home Afloat' (5); 'We Mariners of England' (5); 'Bad Luck at Bendigo', Henry & Joseph Morley (4); 'Among the Shallows' (1); 'The Cradle and the Grave', Hogarth Jr & Morley (4); 'Chip: Voices from the Deep', Morley & an anonymous contributor (5); 'John Chinaman in Australia' (2); 'Britannia's Figures' (2).

Morley, Joseph (1816– date not known) was Henry Morley's brother. Joseph was more conventional and conservative than his younger brother Henry.

According to Joseph Morley's article in *H.W.*, he went to Australia in 1849 (prior to the Victorian gold discoveries) and found, on his arrival, that the letters of introduction he had been given to influential people in Melbourne were of no value as people in Melbourne 'received a great many more drafts upon their courtesy than they could possibly honour.' When gold was found, he decided, with some of his shipmates to try his luck at the diggings. He was unsuccessful and soon returned to England.[42]

– 'Bad Luck at Bendigo', Henry & Joseph Morley (4).

Mr Mulock (not identified). The first and third items listed below are letters (or extracts from letters) that were written by a contributor in 1851, from Geelong to a friend in England. According to the letters and the editorial remarks accompanying them, the contributor was a young man who was a 'recent settler' in Australia.[43] The article states that in partnership with Mr Rumble, he had bought a farm near Mt Swardle (or Swaddle [sic]), an extinct volcano in the Geelong district, described as being a thousand years old. Recent investigations reveal no records of a Mt Swardle (or Swaddle) in the district, or of this name having been used in the past and, according to Assoc. Prof. E.B. Joyce, from the School of Earth Sciences, Melbourne University, the area has many extinct volcanoes, all older than those described in the article.[44]

Lohrli's research indicated that payment for the third item listed as 'handed by Wills,' July 10, was presumably to Mulock's correspondent. It is possible that the noted author and poet, Dinah Maria Mulock, who also contributed to *H. W.*, may have been the person responsible for providing the letters.

– 'Chip: A Bush Fire in Australia' (3); 'The Harvest of Gold' (4); 'We, and Our Man Tom' (2).

Ollier, Edmund (1827–1886) a writer and poet, was the son of Charles Ollier, the prominent publisher of poets such as Keats and Shelley. Edmund Ollier had acted in an editorial capacity at *Leader*, *Atlas* and *London Review* and as a contributor to several periodicals.[45]

He wrote to Dickens in 1850, some ten weeks prior to commencement of the publication of *H. W.*, to ask about the possibility of writing for the new periodical. Dickens' reply suggested that he would not 'pledge himself beforehand, to the acceptance of any article' but that the plans for the 'projected Miscellany' called for the use of good occasional contributions.[46] Ollier contributed fifteen prose pieces to *H. W.* and a further thirty-four poems. It would appear that Ollier's work was 'well appreciated by the illustrious conductor' and in 1852, Dickens himself wrote of Ollier being 'an excellent and true young poet.'[47]

Ollier wrote one poem in relation to Australia, 'The Ballad of the Gold Digger'. This was published at the time when many articles focusing on Australia, particularly on the gold diggings, were being printed in *H. W.* from contributors such as Horne, Hogarth, Michie, Mulock, and Sidney.
– 'The Ballad of the Gold Digger' (4).

Payn, James (1830–1898) was a noted English novelist. Payn was educated at Eton, The Royal Military Academy, Woolwich and Cambridge University. While still an undergraduate Payn started sending verse and prose to periodicals and also published two volumes of verse. He became a close friend of Dickens, and they exchanged many letters. Lohrli states that he was obviously a great admirer of Dickens as his letters made frequent reference to him. She noted that Payn had written that Dickens 'wrote letters as good as his books.'[48] Payn wrote sixty-seven prose articles and one poem for *Household Words.* His article 'The Savage Muse' was a scathing, almost sarcastic criticism of a hugely popular 'poetical narrative' of Kinahan Cornwallis that was in vogue at the time. Cornwallis (1839–1917) had spent time working in Melbourne as a public servant leaving Australia in 1855. He also published prose articles about Melbourne.[49]

According to Payn's article, Cornwallis' poem 'Yarra Yarra, or the Wandering Aborigine', was in thirteen books and in its fifth edition. In the long narrative poem, to which Payn took exception, Cornwallis had apparently professed to detail the life of an Australian Aborigine named Yarra Yarra. Payn deplored Cornwallis' idealised depiction of the Aboriginal, referring to it as 'the noble savage, with a vengeance.' About the time Payn's piece was printed in the periodical Dickens published various others describing experiences with Aborigines (he too was not an admirer of the concept of the noble savage.) The name 'The Savage Muse' has a typical Dickensian title, being a double or, even triple pun.
– 'The Savage Muse' (3).

Rinder, Samuel (1825–1907), businessman and public official in Victoria. Rinder was the son of a Methodist preacher, and was born and educated in Leeds. There is some confusion in relation to his early life history.[50] As a boy

Rinder went to sea as a cabin boy on a vessel sailing between Liverpool and New York. In the early 1840s he was an apprentice on the *Hope of Plymouth*. He sailed to Melbourne and stayed for some years in Tasmania with an uncle. About 1849, he returned to England, having sailed via Peru with the intention of getting to California where gold had recently been found; stayed for about three years, then shipped out again to Melbourne where he started a butcher's business. He then worked for two years carting goods between Melbourne and the Castlemaine diggings. Ever resourceful, Rinder operated a general store, became a grazier, farmer and finally a leading businessman in the Korong district. He was secretary and treasurer of the Korong Shire for forty years and a justice of the peace.

Rinder was an able writer and speaker. In addition to contributing to Victorian newspapers, he wrote eight articles for *H.W.* between 1852 and 1855, five of which related to Australia. Of the eight, Rinder was recorded in five as the sole writer. In the remaining three he wrote in conjunction with Morley. His description of whaling in 'Black Skin A-head!' reads as a first hand narrative that stands the test of time as a descriptive piece. 'We Mariners of England' and 'Sailor's Home Afloat' draw attention to and sharply criticises, the poor working conditions endured by sailors on board English vessels. The criticisms made in 'Sailors Home Afloat', was confirmed in a follow-up letter (published anonymously as a Chip) from 'a master mariner of the Antipodes' in *Voices from the Deep* (reprinted in Book 5).
– 'Black-Skin Ahead!' (5); 'Sailors' Home Afloat' (5); 'We Mariners of England' Rinder & Morley (5); 'Four-Legged Australians' (2); 'Australian Carriers' (4); 'Chip: Voices from the Deep' (5).

Sala, George Augustus Henry Fairfield (1828–1895) was educated in France and England. He was a journalist, essayist, lecturer and editor. From a family of singers and actors, Sala initially earned a living as a scene painter, illustrator and engraver. He met Dickens in 1836 when his mother acted in one of Dickens' plays and, with a 'precocious talent' for writing and drawing, entered early into the London literary society.[51]

In the 1840's Sala started contributing to minor London journals, and in 1851 began writing articles for Dickens' *Household Words.* Dickens' biographer John Forster relates that Sala was regarded by Dickens at the 'highest ranks' to assist him,[52] and as such in 1856, Dickens sent him to Russia to write a number of travel sketches. He wrote nearly 150 articles for *H.W.*, of which two were related to Australia. After a disagreement with Dickens in 1857, Sala started a long association with the *Daily Telegraph* and was sent by the paper to New York, Europe and elsewhere around the globe, including Australia. Sala also published some forty works of fiction and non-fiction—he was a highly entertaining and prolific writer, with a worldwide reputation. After reconciling with Dickens, he later wrote for *All the Year Round.*

Sala visited Melbourne in the 1885. It was he who coined the name 'Marvellous Melbourne,' to capture the wealth and excitement of the city for his newspaper readers in England.[53]
– 'Cheerily, Cheerily!' (2); 'Unfortunate James Daley' (4).

Sidney, John (1821–?), son of physician, Abraham Solomon, and like his brother Samuel, (below) adopted the anglicised surname 'Sidney'. Having completed his education in France and England, John Sidney, at the age of seventeen in 1838, arrived in New South Wales where he raised sheep, cattle and horses in the 'wildest parts of the colony.' He stayed in Australia for six years, leaving for England in 1844.

In 1847, Smith Elder and Co. published, *A Voice from the Far Interior of Australia, By a Bushman*, which was prefaced by the remarks: 'To the magistrates and country gentlemen of England, Scotland and Ireland, these observations are respectfully addressed, by, their obedient humble servant, John Sidney'. According to his brother Samuel, John was a 'close observer, but no writer.'[54] As a result, they co-edited a number of articles and books together including *The Australian Handbook* (1848), followed by *Sidney's Emigrant's Journal* and *Three Colonies of Australia* (1852). He returned to Australia in 1848.

In 1850, John Sidney's 'Milking in Australia' was published in the first issue of *Household Words.* Nevertheless, John's contribution to *H.W.* continued indirectly, as his brother Samuel used information provided by

John as a source of the personal observations and experiences in the articles he wrote (see below).[55]
– 'Milking in Australia' (2).

Sidney, Samuel (1813–1883). The son of Abraham Solomon and like his brother John assumed the surname Sidney. Educated for the law, he worked as a solicitor for a time before turning to journalism and becoming a writer specialising on topics concerning emigration, railways and agriculture—chiefly, livestock. He co-authored a number of books and articles with his brother John (see, above), made speeches on emigration and wrote pamphlets on the subject. He also wrote for *Illustrated London News* as well as a number of journals relating to agriculture and stock. He was an assistant commissioner for the Great Exhibition. The Sidneys' *Australian Handbook* (1848) was extremely popular and sold thousands of copies; as did their *Sidney's Emigrant's Journal* (1848–50). In 1852, Samuel Sidney published *The Three Colonies of Australia*.

Samuel Sidney met Dickens as a result of the prominence he and his brother achieved through their books, pamphlets and speeches. They were regarded as authorities on migration to Australia which Dickens wanted to foster and encourage.

As an illustration of Dickens' desire to acquire accurate information about Australia, even before the discovery of gold, in a letter to Miss Burdette-Coutts, Dickens referred to 'the writers of those pamphlets', and stated that 'he had some time before directed a gentleman' to 'confer with them on the practicality of our doing something useful on the subject of emigration.' Dickens said the books they sent 'gave him knowledge of the state of society in New South Wales of which one could have no previous understanding, and which would seem to be quite misunderstood, or very little known, even in the cities of New South Wales itself.'[56]

Despite having never personally visited Australia, of the sixty articles Samuel Sidney wrote for *H.W.*, seventeen were about Australia. These had been augmented by the substantial correspondence received by Dickens and other members of staff from immigrants to Australia, and especially through personal information supplied by his brother John and others, such as Caroline Chisholm.

– 'Milking in Australia', John Sidney & Samuel Sidney (2); 'An Australian Ploughman's Story' (3); 'Two-Handed Dick the Stockman' (3); 'An Exploring Adventure' (3); 'Chip: Family Colonisation Loan Society' (2); 'Father Gabriel; or, The Fortunes of a Farmer' (3); 'Father Gabriel's Story' (3); 'Two Adventures at Sea' (5); 'Chip: Letter of Introduction to Sydney' (2); 'Christmas Day in the Bush' (3); 'Two Scenes in the Life of John Bodger' (2); 'Three Colonial Epochs' (2); 'Better Ties Than Red Tape' (2); 'Going to the Dogs' (3); 'Chip: What to Take to Australia' (2); 'Chip: Climate of Australia' (2); 'Lost and Found in the Gold Fields' (4); 'Treasures of the Deep' (5); 'Land ho!—Port Jackson' (2).

Thomas, William Moy (1828–1910) journalist, drama critic, novelist and scholar who studied law but soon turned to writing. Thomas contributed articles to numerous periodicals. He was the London correspondent for the *New York Round Table* and was on the staff of *Daily News*, and drama critic for the *Graphic* and *Academy* and other publications.

Lohrli wrote that Dickens was introduced to Thomas in 1850 and soon came to 'think highly of Thomas' ability and judgement.' Furthermore, in discussing Thomas' contribution to *H.W.* she said, 'The social purposes of Dickens' literary works was well understood by Thomas; nine years after Dickens' death he acclaimed and acknowledged Dickens in an article published in *Social Notes*, October 25, 1879.'[57]

Thomas was to write thirty-six articles over the next six years for *H.W.* The one article he wrote relating to Australia was 'Transported for Life'. It is an account of the transportation to Norfolk Island (then to Van Diemen's Land), of William Henry Barber (not named in the article). Barber, a solicitor, had been convicted of complicity in a case of fraud and forgery and had been transported in 1844; he had received a final unconditional pardon in 1848. Lohrli records that the basis of this article was 'probably based on the book *The Case of Mr. W.H. Barber*' and that Dickens had a copy in his library.

Thomas' article in *H. W.*, told in first person, is stated to have 'been taken down from the lips of the narrator, whose sufferings are described; with the object of shewing [sic] what Transportation, at the present time, really is.' Also that W.L. Clay, in (*The Prison Chaplain* p. 215n) referred to the article as 'a painfully interesting narrative' giving 'a good account of Norfolk Island' under the administration of Major Joseph Childs. Certain regulations as recorded in the article were no longer in force at the time it appeared in *Household Words.*[58]
– 'Transported For Life, Parts 1 and 2' (1).

Ullathorne, Rev. William B. The article 'The New Colonists of Norfolk Island', quotes Ullathorne's description of Norfolk Island from his *Catholic Mission in Australia*, first published in 1836. The occasion for reprinting the description was the government's removal, in 1856, of the inhabitants of Pitcairn Island to Norfolk Island. There is no record of who prepared this item for publication in *Household Words.*[59]
– 'The New Colonists of Norfolk Island' (1).

Vincent, Frank (Francis), exact details not recorded however the articles suggest he was born and educated in England, (date unknown). According to his *H. W.* article, Vincent migrated to the Port Phillip district of Australia, 'many years ago when Australia was a vast sheep-walk' and was 'unwilling to settle prematurely' but nevertheless, armed with letters of introduction to several squatters, 'took a tour from one station to another in what later became Victoria.' Eventually, Vincent settled at Gundagai, on the Murrumbidgee River, New South Wales, and brought his 'wife up from Sydney.'[60]

During one of his years of residence (date not firmly established) at Gundagai—'in the late evening of the last day of March,' a flood occurred that inundated the entire Gundagai valley that resulted in the 'loss of several lives.' Lohrli's noted 'there is a record, from 1844 to 1852 of several floods in the area, after which the settlement was moved to a higher site. The flood that is recorded in 'The Waters Are Out' is not the huge flood of June 1852 "the great flood" that resulted in the loss of more than a hundred lives.' The latest date in which the writer mentions in connection with his residence in Australia is 1853, when he visited the goldfields of Victoria.

The *H. W.* office book records payment was made to a Bristol address, in February 1858. So he must have left Australia no later than the latter months of 1857, although he may well have returned to Australia. As Lohrli notes, the *Sands' Country Directory and Gazette of NSW* for 1881–82, (in the Mitchell Library) 'lists a Frank Vincent, newspaper proprietor of Uralla, in the Gundagai district.' She suggests this may have been the *H. W.* contributor.[61]
– 'Coo-ee!' (3); 'John Chinaman in Australia', F. Vincent & Morley (2); 'Australian Jim Walker' (3); 'The Waters Are Out' (3).

Weir, William (1802–1858), lawyer, journalist; educated at Ayr Academy, Scotland and at University of Göttingen. Weir was called to the Scottish bar in 1827 and later became the first editor of the Glasgow *Argus* before moving to London. He contributed to the *Spectator* and was engaged on the staff of the *Daily News* by Dickens where he served as the paper's 'chief authority on railways and commercial affairs'.[62]

Weir contributed four articles to *H. W.* on commerce and transport, literature and law. Whilst not primarily focused on Australia, the two articles included in this collection (written at the advent of steam ships), relate to the pressing needs to develop faster international shipping routes. They highlight the necessity for the Panama and Suez Canals to be built, to thus transform global transport, including shipping to Australia.
– 'Short Cuts Across the Globe: The Panama Canal' (5); 'Short Cuts Across the Globe: The Isthmus of Suez', Weir & W. H. Wills (5).

Whitty, Edward Michael (1827–1860). Whitty was the son of a newspaper editor and was educated at Liverpool Institute, and in Hanover. In 1846 he was a writer in the provincial press. In 1848–49 he wrote the parliamentary summaries for *The Times* and some of his summaries were published in *History of the Sessions 1852–3: A Parliamentary Retrospect*, and in *Governing Classes of Great Britain: Political Portraits*, both published 1854. He was editor of *Northern Whig* in 1857–58.

Whitty died in 1860, having migrated to Melbourne (date uncertain) to work on the Melbourne *Argus*.

'Post To Australia' (April, 1856) is a criticism of the lack of interest the British government had in commerce and trade, and the government's failure to re-establish steamship services (to Australia) that had been discontinued during the Crimean War.[63] Whitty wrote, 'for mercy's sake lets get circumnavigation discussions out of the Circumlocution Office as fast as possible.'

The theme of circumlocution was to be used by Dickens in *H. W.* in an article entitled, 'Nobody, Somebody and Everybody', (30 August 1856) which was directed at the maladministration of the country, and in particular of the Crimean War. The 'Circumlocution Office' emerged again as a major focus of his novel *Little Dorritt*, (which was originally to be called Nobody's Fault). In reference to Dickens' writing, author Peter Ackroyd noted that the notion of circumlocution was to become: 'the whole vast babble of the world, the world of travellers, the world of hypocrisy, [and] the world of imprisonment.'[64]
– 'Post to Australia' (5).

Wills, William Henry (1810–1880), journalist, sub-editor of *H. W.* and later (when it continued under the re-named banner), *All The Year Round*. William Wills was the son of a wealthy shipowner who died when William was quite young. As a result Wills' education was limited, as he was required to financially support his family. He turned to journalism and contributed to several periodicals including, *Penny Magazine*, *Saturday Magazine*, *McCullock's Geographical Dictionary* and *Bentley's Miscellany*. Wills was one of the original literary staff members of *Punch* and contributed to its first issue in 1841. In 1841 he became assistant editor of *Chambers' Journal*, a post he held until 1845.

He married Janet Chambers, and in that same year became Dickens' personal secretary, with the responsibility of helping Dickens to found and edit *Daily News*. He continued to do so until 1849 (even though Dickens had quit *Daily News*). Dickens asked him to be the assistant editor of *Household Words*. Dickens, Forster, Bradbury, Evans and Wills became joint proprietors of *H. W.* (with Wills holding only a small share) on an annual income of £420 per annum, compared to Dickens' £500 pa.

William Wills contributed to 129 issues of *H. W.*, and wrote twenty-eight full-length articles in the first volume alone, but increasingly over the years left more of the writing to other contributors. Nevertheless he wrote or co-wrote a further 178 articles, as well as contributing to many more, in his editing capacity. In the course of his writings, Stone wrote, 'he collaborated with Dickens' more than any other writer.'[65]

Wills was equally responsible with Dickens for the editorial policy and, although *Household Words* bore Dickens' name, in the public's eye Wills' name was nevertheless closely associated. Wills had the responsibility of careful handling of the business transactions of *H. W.*, something to which Dickens was largely indifferent. Wills 'was also responsible for the day-to-day management of the editorial office, carrying on correspondence, conferring with the printers and with contributors and delegating some of the assignments. He referred to Dickens those articles that required Dickens' final decision, and kept the Office Book—a record of items published in *H. W.*, with the amount paid for contributed items.'[66]

Items with an Australian connection that Wills was involved in writing are listed below.

– 'Short Cuts Across the Globe: The Panama Canal', William Weir & Wills (5); 'Short Cuts Across the Globe: The Isthmus of Suez', William Weir & Wills (5); 'Two Letters from Australia', Francis Gwynne & Wills (3); 'Chip: Easy Spelling and Hard Reading', Miss Cox & Wills (2); 'Chip: Safety for Female Immigrants' (2); 'Chip: The Bush Fire Extinguisher', Correspondent & Wills (3); 'Chip: A Golden Newspaper', William Thomas Keene & Wills (4); 'Chip: Official Emigration' (2); 'Chip: Transported for Life' (1); 'First Stage to Australia', Wills & John Capper (2).

Notes

[1] Lohrli, p. 476.

[2] *Australian Dictionary of Biography*, Vol. 4, 1851–90, pp. 221–23.

[3] Lohrli, p. 227.

[4] Lohrli, pp. 226–28.

[5] *Australian Dictionary of Biography*, Vol. 1, p. 222.

[6] Ackroyd, p. 622.

[7] Forster, p. 703.

[8] Murray, p. 68.

[9] Letters of the Dickens Family 1870–1913, National Library of Australia, Manuscripts MS2563.

[10] Lohrli, pp. 269–70.

[11] Lohrli, pp. 290–91.

[12] Lohrli, pp. 303–04.

[13] Lohrli, p. 309.

[14] Lohrli, p. 309.

[15] *Australian Dictionary of Biography*, Vol. 4, 1851–90, p. 424.

[16] Finnane, p. 26.

[17] Keesing, p. 3.

[18] Keesing, p. 56.

[19] Keesing, p. 401.

[20] *Australian Dictionary of Biography*, Vol. 4, 1851–90, pp. 435–36.

[21] Keesing, pp. 401–02.

[22] Lohrli, p. 315.

[23] Lohrli, p. 322.

[24] Gordon, Harry, *An Eyewitness History of Australia*, pp. 55–61.

[25] Lohrli, p. 330.

[26] *Australian Dictionary of Biography*, Vol. 5, 1851–90, pp. 239–40.

[27] *Australian Dictionary of Biography*, Vol. 5, 1851–90, pp. 239–40.

[28] Lohrli, p. 337.

[29] Lohrli, p. 352.

[30] *Australian Dictionary of Biography*, Vol. 5, 1851–90, pp. 239–40.

[31] Lohrli, p. 366.

[32] Significant Tasmanian Women Project, Dept of Premier and Cabinet, Tasmania, www.dpac.tas.gov.au/divisions/cdd/women/leadership/significant_tasmanian_women.
[33] Barber, W.H. *The case of Mr W.H. Barber... : Convicted in 1844 of a Supposed Guilty Knowledge of Certain Will Forgeries, Consisting of His Memorial to Sir James Graham and Other Documents Establishing ... His Perfect Innocence ... with Editorial Remarks* / by Archibald Michie [Sydney?: s.n.], 1847 (Sydney: Kemp and Fairfax).
[34] Lohrli, p. 445.
[35] *Australian Dictionary of Biography,* Vol. 5, 1851–90, pp. 246–48.
[36] Mary Lazarus, *A Tale of Two Brothers: Charles Dickens's Sons in Australia,* p. 19.
[37] Lohrli, p. 367.
[38] *Australian Dictionary of Biography,* Vol.5, 1851–90, pp. 246–48.
[39] Lohrli, p. 367.
[40] Lohrli, p. 370.
[41] Lohrli, p. 370.
[42] Lohrli, p. 380.
[43] Lohrli, p. 380.
[44] Pers. Comm.., Assoc. Prof. E.B. Joyce—School of Earth Sciences, Melbourne University.
[45] Lohrli, pp. 389–90.
[46] Lohrli, p. 390.
[47] Lohrli, p. 390.
[48] Lohrli, p. 399.
[49] Flannery, p. 230.
[50] Lohrli, p. 411.
[51] Stone, p. 659.
[52] Forster, p. 558.
[53] Flannery, p. 326.
[54] Lohrli, p. 429.
[55] Lohrli, p. 429.
[56] Lohrli, p. 430.
[57] Lohrli, pp. 445–46.
[58] Lohrli, p. 446.
[59] Lohrli, p. 479.
[60] Lohrli, p. 452.
[61] Lohrli, p. 452.

[62] Lohrli, p. 455.
[63] Lohrli, p. 460.
[64] Ackroyd, p. 786.
[65] Stone, p. 660.
[66] Lohrli, pp. 460–65.

Bibliography

Australian Dictionary of Biography 1851–1890, Vols. 4 & 5, various eds. Melbourne: Melbourne University Press, 1969–1976.

Ackroyd, Peter, *Dickens*, London: Minerva Paperback, 1991.

Bate, Weston, *Victorian Gold Rushes*, Ringwood, Vic.: McPhee Gribble /Penguin Books, 1988.

Blainey, Geoffrey, *The Rush that Never Ended: a History of Australian Mining*, Melbourne: Melbourne University Press, 1981.

Brown, Ivor, In E.W.F. Tomlin (Ed.), *Charles Dickens 1812–1870: A Century Volume*, London: Weidenfeld and Nicolson Ltd., 1969.

Chesterton, G.K., *Charles Dickens*, London: Methuen & Co. 1906.

Cannon, Michael, *Who's Master? Who's Man? Australia in the Victorian Age*, Melbourne: Currey O'Neil, 1982.

________, *Life in the Country: Australia in the Victorian Age 2*, Melbourne: Currey O'Neil Ross, 1983.

Fido, Martin, *Charles Dickens: An Authentic Account of His Life and Times*, Sydney: The Hamlyn Publishing Group Ltd. n.d.

Finnane, Mark, (Ed.), *The Difficulties of My Position: The Diaries of Prison Governor John Buckley Castieau, 1855–1884*, Canberra: The National Library of Australia, 2004.

Flannery, Tim, (Ed.), *The Birth of Melbourne*, Melbourne: Text Publishing, 2004.

Hancock, Marguerite, (Ed.), *Glimpses of Life in Victoria by 'A Resident'*, Melbourne: The Miegunyah Press, 1996.

Hobsbawm, Eric, *The Age of Capital: 1848–1875*, London: Abacus, 2003.

Hobsbaum, Philip, *A Reader's Guide to Charles Dickens*, London: Thames and Hudson, 1977.

Household Words, 1850–1859, Volumes 1–19, London: Bradbury and Evans, (Vols. 1–3, 5, 7, 11, 17–18), 1850–1858; New York: McElrath & Barker, (Vols. 7–16), 1853–1858; New York: Fredric Brady, (Vol. 19), 1859.

Hughes, Robert, *The Fatal Shore: a History of the Transportation of Convicts to Australia 1787–1868*, London: The Harvill Press, 1986.

Forster, John, *The Life of Charles Dickens, Fireside Edition*, New York: Oxford University Press, n. d.

Johnston, Judith & Anderson, Monica, *Australia Imagined: Views from the British Periodical Press, 1800–1900*, Crawley: University of Western Australia Press, 2005.

Keesing, Nancy (Ed.), *History of the Australian Gold Rushes: By Those Who Were There*, North Ryde, NSW: Angus and Robertson, 1987.

Lohrli, Anne, *Household Words: Table of Contents, List of Contributors and Their Contributions*, Toronto: University of Toronto Press, 1973.

Murray, Brian, *Charles Dickens*, New York: Continuum, 1994.

Pope-Hennessy, Una, *Charles Dickens 1812–1870*, London: Reprint Society, 1947.

Ryan, J.S. & Reed, A.H., *Charles Dickens and New Zealand*, Wellington: A.H. & A.W. Reed, 1965.

Sanderson, Edgar, *The British Empire in the Nineteenth Century*, Vol. VI, London: Blackie & Son, 1898.

Smiley, Jane, *Charles Dickens*, London, Phoenix Paperback, 2003.

Stone, Harry, *Charles Dickens' Uncollected Writings from Household Words, 1850–1859*,Volumes 1 & 2, Bloomington, Indiana: University of Indiana Press, 1968.

Ward, Russel, *Australia Since the Coming of Man*, Sydney: Lansdowne Press, 1982.

Webster's New Twentieth Century Dictionary of the English Language, Unabridged, New York: The World Publishing Company, 1971.

Webster's Third New International Dictionary, Unabridged, Springfield, Mass: Merriam Webster Inc. 1993.

Welles Henderson, J., *Jack Tar: A Sailor's Life 1750–1910*, Woodbridge: Antique Collectors' Club, 1999.

Wilson, Angus, *The Words of Charles Dickens*, London: Martin Secker & Warburg, 1970.

Charles Dickens' Australia
Selected essays from *Household Words* 1850–1859

Researched and presented by Margaret Mendelawitz

Book One: *Convict Stories*, ISBN 9781920898670
Book Two: *Immigration*, ISBN 9781920898687
Book Three: *Frontier Stories*, ISBN 9781920898694
Book Four: *Mining and Gold*, ISBN 9781920899257
Book Five: *Maritime Conditions*, ISBN 9781920899264
Five-Volume Set: ISBN 9781920899271

www.ingramcontent.com/pod-product-compliance
Lightning Source LLC
LaVergne TN
LVHW090953080826
845145LV00003B/998

* 9 7 8 1 9 2 0 8 9 9 2 6 4 *